Gracefully Broken

The Same Storm That Tried To Destroy Me
Became The Gateway To My Purpose

by LaKrystal Lovett

Published by Journey Written ®

Copyright 2021 by LaKrystal Lovett

All rights reserved. No part of this publication may be reproduced, stored in a retrial system, distributed, or transmitted in any form or by any means, including photocopying, recording, or other electric, or mechanical methods, without the prior written permission of the author, this also includes conveying via e-mail without permission in writing by the publisher.

Unless otherwise noted, all Scripture quotations are taken from the Life applications Study Bible NIV. Copyright 1988, 1989, 1990, 1991, 1993, 1996, 2004, 2005, 2007 by Tyndale House Publishers, Inc., Carol Stream, IL 60188. All Rights Reserved.

Disclaimer: While the author believes that the information and guidance in this book are correct, all parties must rely upon their own skills and judgement when making use of it. The author or publisher shall have neither liability nor responsibility to anyone with respect to loss of damage caused by, or alleged to be caused, directly or indirectly by the information contained in this book.

ISBN 13: 978-1-7367389-2-4

Printed in the United States of America

First Printing, 2021

Journey Written ® Book-Writing & Publishing

Visit our website at www.JourneyWritten.com

I dedicate this book to my sister and best friend Shamara "Booby" Saffold.

I could have never imagined living in a world without you. Although life has been a battle, I refuse to throw in the towel. I miss our talks. I miss your laugh and the jokes we shared. You are my reason. You are my motivation. Everything I do is to make you a proud big sister. Even though you're gone, we're still a team. You will live through me forever.

I love you always.

CONTENTS

PREFACE 1
Introduction 3
Preparation 7
   Conviction 7
   The Pruning Season 14
   Let me encourage you 30
   Christian Journey 30
   Let me encourage you 38

Gracefully Broken 41
   "Losing Booby" 41
   Let me Encourage you 50
   Losing myself 52
   Grief, Then 60

Life After Death 67
   The Rebirth 67
   Grief, Now 73

Final Thoughts 75
ACKNOWLEDGMENTS 77
Dealing with Grief: 7 ways to cope 79

PREFACE

If anyone would have told me that I would write a book one day, I would have denied it. In fact, God told me in 2018 that I would be an author. I refused to believe him. I didn't feel qualified. I dismissed the idea with fear and insecurity. I thought: "What would I talk about?" "Who would listen to what I have to say?"

What's that saying? God doesn't call the qualified, He qualifies the called. God can use anybody, even though he is perfectly aware of our weaknesses and incompetence. He is known for making the impossible possible.

I didn't think that I was qualified to write a book when he gave me the vision. The truth is, I was indeed qualified. I just hadn't been called yet.

One day I was spending time with God, and he declared something over my life. He said: There are women who need to hear your story. Someone's deliverance depends on your obedience. He told me that I have souls to save, and I needed to complete the assignment that he had given me (The Book).

Ironically, writing this book has saved my soul. This book is a part of my healing process. Although writing was a challenge for me, the process was therapeutic. With each chapter, I was forced to relive my most devastating memories. Crafting each paragraph took courage and vulnerability. Each word pulled me further away from my comfort zone. In fact, I had writing sessions that quickly turned into crying sessions. But I wouldn't change a thing. I wrote this book because after everything I have been through, I found purpose in my pain. Some people admire my resilience. But I refuse to give myself any of the credit. I owe everything to God. When I was weak, he made me strong. 2 *Corinthians 12:9-10 says, "My grace is sufficient for you, for my power is made perfect in*

PREFACE

weakness."

I want you to understand how God broke me to rebuild me again.

Tasha Cobbs Leonard said it best in her song "Gracefully Broken". She said, "God will break you to position you, break you to put you in your right place, but when he breaks you, he doesn't destroy you, he does it with Grace." Sometimes our greatest tragedies are opportunities for growth. At the lowest point in my life, God rebuilt my character. I am no longer the person that I was. A new version of me has been created. I am a stronger, wiser, more self-aware version of myself. Are you ready to witness how God's power was made perfect in my weakness? Are you ready to discover how I was gracefully broken?

Introduction

It was something about his body language. I could sense his uneasiness. I will never forget the way that he slightly dropped his head as he told us that my best friend was gone. I can still hear the police officers' voices in my head. "She is deceased." Those were the words that changed my life forever.

Chilllleeeee. Listen. My best friend and I did everything together. She was two years older than I was and her name was Shamara aka Booby. Biologically she was my mom's younger sister. But you couldn't tell us that we didn't share the same womb. I mean, you could, but just don't let any one of us hear you say it.

There is this childhood photo of Shamara and I, standing in our grandparents living room. We were dressed casually but I'm not quite sure where we were headed. I'm about two years old, a chubby little face (which I still have), wearing a purple long sleeve bodysuit with a Mickey Mouse jumper, staring confusedly into the camera. Next to me is Shamara. Wearing a pink turtleneck, pink pants, and a multicolored sweater. She had the biggest, most-brightest smile on her face. Now before you judge our clothes let me just start by saying that we were toddlers in the mid 90's. She was about four years old and already playing her role of a protective big sister. Her little arm was wrapped tightly around my neck and her pudgy cheek pressed closely to mine. That is how I remember us. Not as aunt & niece but as sisters who grew up learning to love & protect one another. Booby was a nickname given to Shamara by our late grandfather. Our grandparents are one of the reasons we grew up so close knit. They instilled the importance of God and family. As children, every Friday evening we were eagerly clapping our hands and screaming to the top of our lungs trying to out sing each other during worship. And every Saturday morning (we grew up Seventh Day Adventist) we would try our hardest not to fall asleep in church. Neither of us wanted to be awakened by the sting of our grandmother's horrific pinch. Those were the good ol' days. Some of the best times of my life.

Shamara was more than just a sister, she was my soulmate. It was rare that you would see me without her. And vice-versa. We spent our entire childhood together. She was the Meredith Grey to my Christian Yang. She was my person. When we needed advice, we looked to each other. She would always call me with some tea to spill. Or as we called it "Bitness". Nobody was as loyal as my big sister. If I were in need, she was the first person by my side. Booby was such a loving and outgoing person. Such a joy to be around.

Shamara understood me. We shared some of the best inside jokes. Our bond was strong. And let me just say that big sis did not play about me. I remember one day when we were at work (yes, we worked together) someone asked Booby if I was her "real" sister. Now, anybody that knows Shamara knows that she does not tolerate foolishness. She would throw shade in a minute. But you let somebody try to throw shade her way and it would become a war. When having a conversation with Shamara it was best that you came correct. In other words, watch your mouth or the conversation could go left quickly.

Why on earth did that woman ask if I was Booby's real sister? It was over before it even started. Shamara went OFF! I think her comeback was something along the lines of: "Why are you in my business? Is this a REAL ass whoopin you finna get if you don't get outta my face?". But that was Booby for you. I was used to it. She was sweet and such a fun person to be around. But she didn't take no shit. Ask anybody who has ever spent more than 5 minutes with her.

She didn't like people to be in her business. She wasn't a secretive person - she was private. If she didn't willingly tell you something, then DON'T ask her. The fact that we weren't biological sisters wasn't important. We were family and that's all that mattered. But it seemed like people always had something to say about our relationship. We didn't care. We were sisters. And we would go to war with anybody who thought otherwise.

Shamara was a selfless person. She would do anything for anybody. If she cared for you, she would literally give you the shirt off her back. And she wouldn't expect a thing in return. She did not have to try hard to be caring. It came natural to her. She was born with a heart of gold.

She was a down to earth person with a kind heart. And that naturally drew people to her. She was also hilarious. I'm talking: stomach hurting, tears-streaming-down-your face-because-you-are-laughing-so-hard funny. She was always smiling and laughing. She loved cracking jokes and making other people laugh. You always knew that it would be a good time when Shamara was around. Her confidence made her unique. She was a big girl with an even bigger heart to match. She embraced who she was, flaws and all. She wanted people to know that just because she was a big girl – contrary to what society thinks – didn't mean that she loved herself any less.

She embodied confidence. She wore it like a badge of honor. And Booby wasn't afraid to let the world know that she loved herself, every chance that she got. Anytime you were in her presence you could feel a genuine connection. My sister encouraged others to love themselves as she loved herself. She loved the people close to her. Not just her family but also her co-workers and friends because they had become her family as well.

I am so blessed to have known her. I am so grateful to have experienced such pure love. Such greatness. Such authenticity. Shamara was truly a gift from God. She was a woman who everybody loved. So many people connected with her. She was the type of person that I wanted to be. The person that could light up a room. The person that constantly put others before herself.

She taught me what it means to embrace who you are. I think people adored her because she always brought the same gorgeous smile and genuine aura. My sister would walk into a room and demand your attention. Not by forcing it. But by making you laugh and capturing your heart. She was gorgeous. And she still had that captivating smile that she wore when we were kids. Shamara was amazing. The bond that we shared was one of a kind.

That's why when I heard the officer tell me that Shamara was dead, I was confused. I couldn't understand why this happened to her. My first thought was: "Deceased?" Are you sure?" Maybe there has been a mistake.

It felt surreal. I didn't want to believe it. When I woke up the morning of June 1st, 2019, I had no idea that my life was getting ready to change forever.

Preparation

Conviction

January 1, 2019

Journal entry

As I reflect on 2018, I officially declare myself a warrior. I faced so many hardships this past year. So many things tried to break me. But one thing I did not do was give up. I learned a lot about myself. I have come far, and I do not give myself enough credit for that. My biggest challenge in 2018 was what I called my "Quarter Life crisis". That was the hardest thing to pull myself out of. I stopped believing in myself. I let overthinking take over my life. I felt like I was not where I should be in life according to my age. I panicked. 2018 has taught me to trust the process. I learned to believe in myself even when I felt like I wanted to give up. I am a queen who deserves everything that my heart desires. The past year has been difficult. I am glad that it is over. I have had disappointments. Setbacks. And even a heartbreak but I made it through. It is time for me to accomplish some goals. It's time to take better care of myself physically and mentally. I need to focus solely on myself. I know that this year will be a wonderful one for me. I am ready to work hard and change my mindset. I will create a new lifestyle. I will take better care of my finances. I will get the life that I deserve.

    It was January of 2019, and I was relieved. 2018 had finally come to an end. Mentally I was drained. I felt like the past year had chewed me up and spit me out. I desperately wanted to detach from the world. I felt like my spirit needed cleansing. And like everybody else in the world at the beginning of a new year, I felt like 2019 was giving me a fresh start.

I was home one morning, cleaning the kitchen. As I scrubbed the pots and pans, Mary J Blige's song My Life blared through my headphones. Life can be only what you make it, when you're feeling down you should never fake it. I was getting ready to join Mary and sing along, when suddenly my music was interrupted by a text message.

The text was from Marlena - my aunt who is more like a sister. She sent me a podcast that she wanted me to listen to. It was a sermon by Sarah Jakes Roberts. After opening the message, I thought, "Another sermon, I'll watch it later". And then I proceeded to sing along with Auntie Mary. But something urged me to listen to the sermon at that moment. I was hesitant at first, because I wasn't in the mood to hear anybody preaching. I just wanted to clean up and listen to my music. Both are therapeutic for me. But as I finished the dishes, I decided to let the podcast play while I cleaned the stove.

Pastor Sarah's sermon read me like a book. She spoke about people who had strayed away from God. She specifically targeted the people who knew God but somehow got out of alignment with him. She said, "Even you, Jesus still loves you." Now to some people that may not mean anything. But those words meant everything to me. It's one thing for a sermon to speak directly to your situation. But it's another thing when it happens unexpectedly. I played the podcast in hopes of hearing a good message. I was not expecting her words to captivate me. She also spoke about not being afraid to let God back into your life. Suddenly, I realized that I was caught up in my own life. So caught up, that I had lost sight of who God is. I grew up in church, so I've known God my entire life. But I've never had a real relationship with him. He was more like an acquaintance than a friend. I was halfway through the sermon and I started to feel convicted. Conviction can be defined as the feeling of being convinced of a wrongdoing or a sin. At the time, I knew nothing about conviction. What I understood was the guilt that I felt. I knew that I was a sinner. But up until that point, I was okay with the way that I was living. I knew that I wasn't living for Christ. And suddenly, I felt a strong urge to repent. I needed to ask God for forgiveness. I felt that I needed to change my ways and live according to his rules. I needed to build a relationship with God. It was the most bizarre thing that I have ever experienced. Too unbelievable to put into words. The bible says, as it is, I rejoice, not because you were grieved but because you were grieved into repenting. For you felt a Godly grief so that you suffered no loss through us. For Godly grief produces a repentance that leads to salvation without regret, whereas worldly grief produces death. 2 Corinthians 7:9-10

At some point in time, between my failures and life's disappointments, I stopped focusing on God. I started to doubt his existence. I kept thinking about how disappointed my grandparents (God rest their souls) would be if they knew that I had given up on Christ.

2018 took me on a rollercoaster ride. Full of hardship. I was too busy dealing with life's struggles to give God my undivided attention. I was broken. I had no direction. I knew that I wanted better for myself. I just didn't know where to start. The funny thing is, while I was making my new year plans, God had his own new year resolution for me. And I had no idea.

Prayer Journal Entry

January 3, 2019

Lately, I have been feeling like nothing is working in my favor. Yesterday I read a book by Cora Jakes Coleman called Faithing It. I also listened to a podcast and said a prayer. That made me feel so much better. It was the best thing that I could have ever done for my mood. It was so soothing to my soul. I'm starting to wonder how much easier life would be if I prayed more? Prayer is so powerful. Trusting God and believing that he will see me through the tough times is important. From this day forward I want to start each day with prayer and journaling. I am on a new path and I pray that the Lord will help me adopt this new habit of faith and prayer. I want to be consistent with my prayer and faith. 2019 will be the year of transformation. I will transform my mindset. How I perceive things is important. God will cover me and help me with my transformation. I have been having an urge to stop dating. I feel like I should listen to this feeling. I believe that it is for a specific reason. I can do this lord. I can transform my life. I can build a relationship with you. I am a Kings kid. I can do all things through Christ who strengthens me.

The bible says in Matthew 7:7, ask and it shall be given, seek, and ye shall find, knock and it shall be opened unto you. I was new to prayer life. I had no idea that when you pray, you must be ready to receive what you prayed for. And you must be willing to accept everything that comes with it. This experience showed me just how powerful prayer is. Be careful what you pray for. Or better yet, make sure that you are ready to receive what you pray for. After being convicted, I slowly started to build a relationship with God. I had no idea what I was doing. I started with journaling. And then asking God to help me understand what was happening in my life. I wanted to be closer to him. I wanted to have faith. I wanted to understand the urges that I was feeling. The Holy Spirit started to speak to me. I didn't know it was the Holy Spirit at the time. The feeling was more like an urge in the pit of my stomach. It was weird. I felt like it could be God, but I wasn't sure. My first instructions were to stop dating. When I first got the urge, I thought: "Nah, that ain't what I heard, maybe I'm tripping." I had recently started dating a guy. He was so gorgeous. We hadn't been dating a full month yet. And suddenly, I got the urge to stop dating and be alone for a while. I did not want to stop dating. How was I supposed to just cut him off? I'm so dramatic and extra. Whenever I meet a new guy and I start to really like him I start planning our wedding. And picking our children's names. I know I can't be the only one don't judge me. Sis really thought she was about to start living her best life. But the Holy Spirit was like: nah sis you down there being ghetto. Getting ready to ruin ya life. (Okay, so the Holy Spirit didn't really say that but that's what it felt like).

I tried fighting the urge. But it became overwhelming. It's like when you want to do something but everything in your spirit is telling you not to do it. That's how I felt.

Cutting that man off was hard. I was sick. I thought: "dang what if he's my husband?"

My next thought was: "okay, how am I going to cut him off? Should I ghost him? Nah, that's childish. Just tell him." I thought: oOkay, I'll just tell him that God told me to cut him off." Then I thought, "nah, you can't say that because then he'll think you're crazy." At the time, I was embarrassed. I didn't want anybody to know that I was building a relationship with God. It's one thing for me to say that I believe in God. But I didn't want anybody to know that I was hearing the Holy Spirit. Where I am from, most people don't just walk around telling each other what God told them to do. Especially if you're talking to a person whose belief is not as strong as yours. They'll probably look at you like you're crazy. I couldn't lose my boo and possibly be labeled crazy. Ultimately, I decided to send the guy a text message. I basically told him that he was a nice guy, but I needed to work on myself. The ol "It's not YOU, It's ME" scenario. He was confused. And he kept asking me questions. That made breaking things off a little harder. But eventually, he accepted my decision. Afterwards I was frustrated. I couldn't understand why God wanted me to stop dating. I didn't want to be alone. That night in my prayers I said, "I don't understand the meaning of this God but help me to trust you anyway." Looking back, I realize that all things were working together for my good. God is intentional. He knew that dating wasn't good for me at the time. I was dating with no purpose. Our situation was based on sex. We weren't adding value to each other's lives. We weren't working towards a relationship. I wouldn't even call it dating. But for a lack of a better term, I'll just leave it at that. I knew that God's plans for me were better than my own. Especially since I wouldn't lose anything by breaking things off with the guy.

Journal entry

January 2019

Dear Lord, I come to you humble and vulnerable, and I ask that you walk with me through my tough journey. I am trying so hard to do your will and believe in you. I need your help, Father, because I cannot do this alone. I am so sorry that I started to doubt you and not believe in your will. I am in a weak state of mind. I need you now more than ever. I need you to strengthen my faith. I need you to make me a believer. I want to trust you even when times get hard, and it seems like you are no longer with me. I need for you to help me love myself, I need for you to help me love you more each day. I know that this will be a process. I know that there will be obstacles along the way. But I am ready. I pray against my doubts. I pray that I can stop doubting my ability to obey you. I am a child of God. There is nothing that I can't do.

I love you.

Amen.

My transition from living my way to living God's way started with the help of Marlena. She was in the process of building a relationship with God. I believe that God used her to get through to me. She would send me scriptures daily. And sermons that she recommended that I watch. She would call me, and we would discuss her daily routine with God. Marlena would remind me of the 10 commandments. And other stories from the Bible that we read as children. Stories such as David and Goliath and Moses and the burning bush. The stories never seemed that interesting when we were younger. But she made them seem so intriguing. I was surprised to learn that the people from the bible were experiencing the same struggles that I was facing as an adult. I was so interested in learning for myself. But I didn't own a bible. The only thing that I was reading at the time was Faithing it a book by Cora Jakes Coleman (Bishop T.D Jakes eldest daughter). I read that book religiously. Every chapter spoke directly to me.

Between Cora's book and Marlena's encouragement, I was inspired to create my own daily routine with God. I would wake up, pray, and journal. I would take the scriptures that Marlena would send me along with the prayers that she would create, and I would study them. Then I would pray to God and ask for understanding. I journaled my thoughts. I journaled what I was grateful for. And the things that I needed God to help me with. I watched at least one sermon a day. Eventually I found my grandfather's bible and started to use it. I was so excited to incorporate reading God's word into my routine with him. Marlena became my accountability partner. She kept me on track. Whenever things got difficult, she was there to encourage me to trust God. She showed me how to understand the stories in the bible. I am forever grateful for her.

Journal Entry

January 2019

I am so thankful for Marlena, we have been through a lot and so many times I wanted to throw our relationship away, but I am so glad that I didn't. She has been supportive and encouraging especially when I feel myself slipping. I am so thankful for her and our experiences. She has taught me so much about trusting you God. Believing in you and myself. She's a good friend and listener. I don't think I can get through this next year without her. Our relationship has grown, we've become a lot closer. I lean on her for support, and I am thankful that I have her in my life.

Shortly after I stopped dating, the Holy Spirit instructed that I enter an alone season. An alone season for me, meant purposely dedicating my time to God to grow closer with him. I learned that during an alone season God can reveal your purpose. He shows you your identity in Christ. He strengthens your faith and builds your character. But you must read and obey his word for him to do so. James 1:22 NIV says: Do not merely listen to the word and so deceive yourselves. Do what is said. The distractions in my life included things like sex, alcohol, and purposeless dating. I had been living and making decisions according to my flesh. The Holy Spirit insisted that I start to live and make decisions according to my spirit. I was of the world and instant gratification was my closest friend. Jesus wanted better for me. He wanted me to be more like him. It was hard obeying God because I disagreed with him. He wanted me to stop doing the very things that I loved. I couldn't understand: why me? Why right now? I was frustrated. I did not want to give up my old habits. Everybody around me was doing the same things I was being told NOT to do. I felt like God didn't want me to have fun. Sin was everywhere. It became difficult for me to be obedient. I felt so much pressure trying to obey God. Especially living in this sinful world.

    I started checking google university for what God says about living a life of sin. I was led to an interesting scripture. Galatians 5:16-19 NIV says, So I say, walk by the spirit, and you will not gratify the desires of the flesh. For the flesh desires, what is contrary to the spirit, and the spirit what is contrary to the flesh. They conflict with each other so that you are not able to do whatever you want. But if you are led by the spirit you are not under the law. The acts of the flesh are obvious: sexual immorality, impurity and debauchery, idolatry, and witchcraft; hatred, discord, jealousy, fits of rage, selfish ambition, dissensions, factions and envy; drunkenness, orgies, and the like. I warn you as I did before that those who live like this will not inherit the kingdom of God. Each time I came across some information from Google I would check the Bible. I had to make sure that what I was reading was true. Whenever I became confused about anything, I went to God in prayer. I asked for clarification. If he wanted me to follow Christ, I would need guidance. My relationship with God didn't happen overnight. It took time and patience. The Bible is the blueprint for how we should live our lives. It's full of the do's and don'ts of life. Little did I know, I would need the bible to be the foundation of my relationship with God.

The Pruning Season

During my alone season, I spent a lot of time reading God's word. Learning about his love: how he carried himself, how he forgave others, how he was tempted by Satan in the wilderness (Matthew 4:1-11). How he was betrayed by his own friends. (Luke 22) How he gave others courage when they did not feel qualified. (Exodus 3:1-15)

Reading the Bible helped me understand Jesus and the life that he wants his people to live. One of my favorite things to do was to watch online sermons. One day, I was watching a sermon and a pastor talked about being aware of false prophets. I had never even thought about that before. I was oblivious to the fact that people could be teaching things that are not in the Bible as well as things that don't align with God's word. After watching that sermon, I went to God in prayer about each pastor that I had been allowing to lead me. I asked God to help me stay in alignment with him. It was still early in my journey and I didn't have the ability to decipher between a true prophet and a false prophet. One thing I did know is that Satan was sneaky. And I did not want to be led astray.

During my time alone with God I also did online Bible studies. I came across so many interesting topics. Baptism weas a topic that I came across frequently. It would always cross my mind, but I didn't feel like I was ready. I didn't think that I knew enough about God to be baptized.

However, I did find a church near my home. I became a frequent visitor. It was such an amazing feeling. The closer I grew to God the more I wanted to be in his presence. I wanted everybody to know what God was doing in my life. So, I started telling my family and friends about my new way of living. I learned how to trust in the Lord. Proverbs 3:5-6 says Trust in the Lord with all your heart and lean not on your own understanding.

Trusting God came from being in his presence and spending time with him. I spent time in prayer with him every single day. Our relationship was transparent. It was nothing that I withheld from Jesus. He knows everything anyway. I had no choice but to be honest with him.

I became more cautious of my actions. I monitored everything that I fed my mind and spirit. I focused on the things that helped me become less of the world and more like Christ. If I knew that something would cause me to sin, I would not do it. If I knew that something would tempt me to have sex, I wouldn't entertain it. I became intentional about obeying God. I stopped listening to secular music. Not because religion says that secular music is wrong, but because it was contradicting to the live that I was trying to live. It wasn't worth it.

I stopped watching certain movies and television shows for that same reason. I even stopped putting myself in certain environments that I knew would lead to wrong decision making. I was asking God to help me fight temptation. It was difficult fighting off the desires of the flesh. But I knew that if I was serious about living for God, I had to put forth effort. Why would I place myself in an environment with liquor when I know that I'm trying to stop drinking? Why would I watch a movie that I know has sex scenes if I'm trying to abstain from sex? I heard a pastor by the name of Dharius Daniels say, "some things we don't have to PRAY away if we just STAY away."

Temptation was coming at me left and right. That included drinking. I was trying hard to stay away from alcohol. I know myself. And I knew drinking would only lead to bad decision making like drunk calling my ex. And we all know the purpose of drunk calling. I couldn't allow myself to go backwards. I had come too far.

Prayer Journal Entry

January 2019

Today I feel like I need your help, Lord. I need help getting rid of my soul ties. I cannot do this on my own. I cannot fight my sexual desires on my own. Lord, please remind me of why I started this alone season. My walk with Christ is more important than anything. I am not ready to date right now. A part of me wants the attention and the pleasure. But I am not ready mentally. I am still trying to figure myself out. Lord, I come to you humble and vulnerable. I ask that you please help me to love myself. Help me to be aware of the things that are bad for me. I know that I can do this. With your help Lord I can do anything

In this season, I gained self-control. I held myself accountable for my actions. I was mindful of the things that I did so that I would not be tempted to sin. It was difficult but it worked. I was at my best when I was obeying God.

Overtime, I learned how to communicate with the Holy Spirit confidently. In several different ways: through my inner voice, some people call it their conscience; through other people like family, prophets, even strangers. God also communicated with me through dreams, as well as through sermons and gospel music. To hear from God you must be receptive. It took me a while. At first, I was unable to decipher between the Holy Spirit and my own voice. One thing that I realized is that the Holy Spirit will not tell you to do anything that does not align with God's word. Whenever I got bored and thought about resorting to my old habits something would tell me to get in God's word. When I would stress, I always felt the urge to pray about it instead of worry. That was the Holy Spirit communicating with me. I started making a habit of doing the opposite of what my flesh wanted me to do. This is how I learned to confidently hear from God. He helped me to surrender and be confident knowing that he was in control of my life. Besides a little temptation, trusting God didn't seem too hard. Or so I thought. Seems like the closer I grew to God. The more my faith was tested.

One early morning, I was driving home from work. I jumped on I-96 headed toward Southfield freeway. No sooner than I could switch lanes, I saw a police car. My heart sank. Even though I kept my composure I was nervous. I had been driving on a suspended license for about four years - don't judge me. No sooner than I could get on the freeway the officer whipped behind me. It was over. I knew that I was going to jail.

I was right: he explained why he pulled me over. Asked me to step out of the car. He read me my rights. And I spent the next 4 hours in a holding cell. That was the longest four hours of my life. And such a degrading experience. I made a promise to myself that I would get my license back. And that I would never put myself in a position like that again.

When I got home later that morning, I was so angry with God. Things had been going smooth in my life. Why would he allow this to happen? And then I was reminded by the Holy Spirit not to complain but to be grateful. I wasn't trying to hear that. When I get mad my anger must subside on its own. I can't stand for somebody to try and help me see the good in a situation. Sounds crazy right? The point is I'll calm down eventually but let me be mad first. The holy spirit brought to my attention that I didn't have to stay in jail overnight (Thanks Booby). My car wasn't impounded even though I was driving on a suspended license and without insurance. And despite my hectic day I was reminded that I was still alive, well, and safe.

After being given a pep talk by the Holy Spirit, my perspective changed. Instead of complaining, I started to count my blessings. I instantly snapped out of my pity party. I even surprised myself at how I managed to focus on the good in the situation.

Journal entry

January 2019

Today was not a good day. I was arrested on my way home from work for driving on a suspended license. I am so tired of life right now. Nothing is working in my favor. I cannot win without losing. But one thing I will do is keep my faith. I will not stop believing in God and the fact that he has my back. He did not bring me this far to leave me. I know that something greater is coming for me and my family. It is our job to be patient and obedient in this time of hardship. I will not quit. I want to praise you Lord even at my lowest point. Things could have been worse. I am free. I am healthy. I have friends and family that love and support me. There is no way that I can be ungrateful and complain about anything right now. Everything happens according to God's timing. When he is ready for me to thrive and flourish, I will. Right now, he is testing my obedience. My job is to learn from this and get serious about getting my license back. I cannot afford to put it off any longer. Something magnificent is coming my way. I don't know what it is but a blessing is coming my way.

A few days before I got arrested, I was asking God to transform my life. I was praying that he would help me change my mindset. And accomplish some goals. Getting my license back was a goal that I had been putting off for years. Maybe this was God's way of helping me get my life in order. I couldn't transform overnight but this was a start.

After being arrested, I was so terrified to get behind the wheel of any car. The four hours in that holding cell had me scared straight. There was no way that I would be driving without a license again. I wondered how I would get back and forth to work. I wondered how much it would cost for my license to be reinstated. I was starting to stress. So, I went to God in prayer.

Philippians 4:6 says: do not be anxious about anything, but in every situation, by prayer and petition present your request to God. I prayed that he would make a way for me. Prayer has become second nature to me. And it was so much easier than worrying. I asked God what he wanted me to do. I did not want to move unless his he told me to. I prayed for guidance. Wisdom and instruction.

Ironically, after seeking guidance from the Holy Spirit I felt the urge to quit my job. I was a CNA (Certified nurse aide) working at a nursing home. I hated my job. I have been a CNA since I was eighteen years old. Going on eight years at the time. The job paid the bills, but it didn't fulfill me. I enjoyed working in the medical field. But I knew it wasn't my purpose in life. My initial reaction when I was told to quit my job was "YESSSS!!". But then I thought, this is just me being crazy. I disliked the job but not enough to quit. Besides, that job was my only source of income. How would I get the money to pay for my tickets and get my license back? I tried telling myself that quitting my job was a crazy idea. But the urge grew stronger. The Holy Spirit spoke to me yet again. I was told to trust God. I was told to trust that God had a better job in store for me. Even though I was hesitant I trusted him and I quit my job.

Over time my relationship with God continued to grow stronger. He became my best friend. Since I wasn't working, I had more time to spend with him. I believed that God would provide for me and bless me with an even better job. But my faith quickly turned into fear as time went on. I lived at home with my mom. But I was still responsible for my cell phone bill, my car note, and now my tickets and court fees. Only God knows how much they were going to be. Not to mention the fact that I wanted to pay Shamara back for bailing me out. Just thinking about all the money that I owed worried me. I had no idea what I was going to do. I had no idea how I would continue to pay a car note each month without a steady income. I didn't know how I was going to pay my cell phone bill let alone pay my tickets off. I was starting to regret my decision to quit my job. How could I be so stupid? I didn't think the decision through. After I had enough of letting the devil mess with my mind. I went to God in prayer.

My faith in the Lord was starting to scare me. Even though I was filled with fear, doubt, and regret, I never stopped relying on God. At this point I was frustrated. But I went to him anyway. I didn't go to him like I usually had. I wasn't trying to be cute, and I didn't have time to be fancy. I needed the Holy Spirit to know how I truly felt. Before I gained an actual relationship with Christ, I thought my prayers had to be perfect. I would spend so much time trying not to say the wrong thing. Until I learned that God does not care about that. Prayers do not need to be perfect. They just need to be genuine and from the heart. Matthew 6:5-8 says, and when you pray, do not be like the hypocrites, for they love to pray standing in the synagogues and on the street corners to be seen by others. But when you do pray, go into your room, close the door, and pray to your father, who is unseen. Then your father, who sees what is done in secret, will reward you. And when you pray, do not keep babbling like pagans, for they think they will be heard because of their many words. Do not be like them, for your father knows what you need before you ask him.

Preparation

I went to the Holy Spirit and I said: look I need you so what's up? What do you want me to do? You see me worrying Lord. I have bills that are still due. I have a warrant that may be issued for my arrest if I don't go to court and pay these tickets off. I'm overwhelmed and I'm frustrated. What should I do? The next instruction that God gave me upset me even more.

Not only did he refuse to give me a solution to my problem, now. But he asked me to make another sacrifice. God said, I hear you and I understand your frustration, but I need you to let your car go. I was so annoyed. How was letting my car go going to solve my issues? If anything, it would add to the problem. I said: excuse me? Let my car go? Let my car go where? I came to you for a money solution, God. You asked me to give up dating. I gave up my boo. You asked me to give up my sinful ways. I gave up the sex and drinking. I felt like that video of Tyrese on Instagram "What more do you want from me." I said, there is no such thing as "Letting my car go." It's called repossession. Ain't no way you are telling me to let the finance company repossess my car. That doesn't make any sense at all. What am I supposed to drive? I was already starting to feel worthless because I wasn't working. I had no source of income and more bills than money. And now you want me to be on foot? Then God asked me: how will you pay the note on the car without a job? How will you drive the car without a license? Didn't you say that you were afraid to get behind the wheel of the car because you didn't want to risk being pulled over again? Where do you have to go with no job and no money? Let the car go.

I said: but that will look terrible on my credit. I'll still owe the finance company money. Let the car go. I will provide you with another car trust me, he said. I cried for about 30 minutes after being given those instructions. I needed a money solution, not instructions to make another sacrifice. I didn't want a new car, I wanted the car that I already had. I had my doubts. Deep down I felt like I was making a huge mistake. I had steered myself wrong on several occasions in the past. But God had yet to steer me in the wrong direction. He had yet to forsake me. With fear and anxiety screaming on the inside of me I let my car go. I thought following God meant that I would receive blessings on blessings. I thought my cup was supposed to be overflowing. It didn't seem that way to me. Because my cup was empty. Forget the thought of blessings overflowing. I felt like my blessings hadn't even started coming in yet. And it didn't take long for the devil to get in my head. Satan: you're better off operating in your own strength. At least then you would have a car, job and money. You're better off without the Holy Spirit. God has caused you more harm than good, he said. Following God was starting to hurt. I was uncomfortable. The enemy fed me those lies, and I began to second guess myself.

Once you get into alignment with God and you surrender your life to him. You realize that you are not capable of operating in your own strength anymore. Because certain things in life are too overwhelming for us to handle by ourselves. I had no choice but to let God's will be done over my life. The decisions that he had me making I could not make in my own strength. Because what he had me doing seemed impossible. Trying to operate in my own strength with a decision that God told me to make wouldn't work. It was best that I allow God to lead me. I learned quickly that God won't give you a vision without provision. Everything was already worked out. I was too busy panicking to understand that.

After my car was repossessed, I felt like a complete failure. It may sound strange, but I felt naked without a stable job and a car. I always felt that if I had those things (including money) that I was on the right path in life. I wrapped my identity up in my money, my employment, and my vehicle. It's how I measured my success. I considered those the bare minimum. How did I go from having the bare minimum to not have the bare minimum? Why was God doing this to me? After feeling sorry for myself long enough. I decided to read God's word. The Bible says that God will never leave nor forsake me. (Deuteronomy 31:6) It says that he has plans to prosper me and not to harm me. (Jeremiah 29:11) I had to believe that no matter how my circumstances looked, that God would make a way for me. I needed to stand on the promises that God made me.

When I gave up my job, he told me that he would bless me with a better job. And when I gave up my car, he told me that he would bless me with another one. I needed to have faith in God's promises. Whenever God asks you to make a sacrifice, have confidence in knowing that he will provide. Usually when I made sacrifices, I always received something better in return. But not without me doing the work. A lot of people think that God is a genie. They think that they can say a prayer and what they pray for will magically fall into their laps. But that is not how God works. James 2:17 says, faith by itself, if it is not accompanied by action, is dead. You must believe that God will give you the desires of your heart, but you must also put in the work. Be the type of person to say a prayer and then go get what you prayed for. Having full confidence that God has your back. And knowing that it is already yours.

You're probably thinking: what's the point of prayer? The prayer is for faith. The prayer is for protection. The prayer is so that you are covered. The prayer is so that when you're out there trying to get what you prayed for nothing stands in your way. Nothing hinders you from getting what your heart desires.

The job that God promised me was not going to magically appear. I had faith that the Lord would bless me with a job. But I also did my part. I did the work that it would take to get a new job. I prayed for the job before I ever received it. I prayed that I would like it. I prayed for my future coworkers. I prayed for the environment that he would be placing me into. And then I did the work. I updated my resume. And I applied for every job that my CNA license qualified me for. Once I landed an interview, I made sure to prepare myself. I researched the company so that I would be knowledgeable. I came up with questions for the interviewer. I told myself that even if I did not get the job, I would leave the interview knowing that I did my best.

On the day of my interview, I was full of confidence. I claimed the job well before I was offered the position. In my mind the job was already mine. Being in alignment with God comes with a certain level of confidence. You become so content with who you are. I am a child of God. Therefore, if I pray for something and I get it, great. But if I pray for something and I don't get it, that's cool too. Because I know that God will provide for me regardless. Before the interview, I said a prayer on my way into the building. And before the interview started, I declared "This job is already mine." I repeated that several times while waiting in the lobby for the interviewer. I was extremely nervous during the interview process, but I pushed through. Afterwards, I got home and decided to relax for a while. Not even 2 hours had passed, and I received a call from the recruiter offering me the position. I was ecstatic. I could not thank God enough. I knew that without him none of this was possible.

Getting a new car was a blessing of mine that didn't come as quickly as the new job. But a few months later God blessed me with a new car just as he said he would. After receiving a blessing that God promised me, I always feel guilty for doubting him. His track record is unmatched. In Genesis chapter 15, God promised Abraham that he would have a son. The circumstances didn't look promising for Abraham and his wife Sarah, due to their old age. According to the Bible Abraham was 75 years old when God told him to leave his homeland. After that God promised Abraham a son. Isaac (Abraham's son) wasn't born until he was 100 years of age. The point I am trying to make is never put a time limit on the promises of God. Whenever he says that he will do something, trust that he will surely get it done. He didn't bless me with a car when I wanted it. But when I received it, it was right on time.

Prayer Journal entry

January 2019

Today I received the most exciting news. I was offered a new position. I just want to thank you Lord for this opportunity. I am not worthy of your blessings. My God you are awesome. I stayed faithful. I prayed. I trusted you and your process. And you worked it out for me. I could cry right now. I cannot wait to start my position. You did not bring me this far to leave me. You are on my side. What is for me, will be for me. I am grateful. Thank you so much God. I love you more and more each day. I ask that you continue to take away my doubts and fears. Help me to continue to trust and believe in you. I do not ever want to lose your love. I pray that our relationship grows stronger. I want you to know that I will not give up on you Lord, just because you got me what I wanted. I will not forsake you lord. You have brought me so far in my journey. There is no way that I could ever leave you or go astray. I want you to continue to work on me. I still need you lord like I did in the beginning. Reassure me that you will forever walk with me and be my guide. I am honestly afraid of what my life would be like without you. I am still vulnerable. I still need you. Continue to make me a believer. I want my faith to be stronger than ever. I want to be in tune with you Jesus. So that I know when something is not sent by you. Nobody loves me like you do. I am so glad that our relationship is growing. I love you always.

Your daughter,

LaKrystal.

I was learning that everything was according to God's will. If it was meant to happen for me, it would. I learned to "Cast my worries and anxiety upon the Lord." 1 Peter 5:7 God did just what he said he would. He blessed me with a better job. I was blessed with a higher salary. And the job offered more convenient work hours. God knew what I needed more than I did. I was happier than I had been in a long time.

Of course, it was easy for me to trust God when everything that started off bad ended up working in my favor. Of course, it was easy to be obedient when the Lord was answering my prayers. How many of us can trust God when things do not work in our favor? Or when things do not look promising. Is it easy to trust God when we do not get our way? Or when he is taking too long to answer a prayer. I wrote in my journal at the beginning of January and said "I want to be able to trust the Lord at all times, even when I do not get the things that I want. I want my faith to be stronger than ever." Little did I know another test was coming to see if I truly meant what I was praying to the Lord for.

I was so excited about my new job offer that I almost forgot about my tickets. I was reminded when I received a letter in the mail. The letter stated that I had a court date coming up. I had a job now, but I still didn't have much money. So, I decided that I would skip the court date. I figured I had gone this long without having a license. A little while longer wouldn't hurt. I'll be fine, I thought. So, what – they'll put another warrant out for my arrest. They'll have to catch me first. It's funny how I was trying to live for God but lowkey still trying to do things my way. I was too anxious to start work to worry about a court date. I took the letter that I got in the mail and shoved it in my drawer. I thought: I'll deal with it one day. Just not anytime soon.

One day I was laying across the couch doing a Bible study about baptism. It had been on my mind off and on, but I still didn't feel qualified. Suddenly I got a phone call from the job recruiter. I thought she'd already given me my start date and I had already taken my physical and drug screening. What could she be calling for? After our brief conversation, I hung up the phone feeling defeated yet again. She was calling to tell me that I did not pass my background check. And as a result, she may have to remove my job offer. I had no idea what could have caused me to fail my background check. I didn't smoke so it couldn't have been a failed drug screening. I didn't have a criminal history. So, what could it be?

All that she could tell me was that my background check showed that I was under open investigation by law enforcement. I had no idea what that meant but I figured it had to have something to do with my license. That was the only thing I could think of. I thought I was slick. I thought I was about to get out of paying my tickets for at least a few months. The law is confusing to me. I thought: how does an arrest warrant for traffic violation show up on a background check? I knew it was a crime. But I didn't think it was that serious. I was wanted for

Preparation

driving without a license. My mentality back then was, it's not like, God forbid, I was a murderer or a thief. I became so irritated. I could not believe it. I was trying to move forward but it seemed impossible. I asked the recruiter, "Is there anything that I could do to secure the job?" She told me that to do so I must get the matter cleared up a week before my start date. I was under pressure. But I worked hard to get this job. And I was determined not to let anything get in my way.

I immediately called the court. I needed to get the warrant cleared as soon as possible. After speaking with the clerk at the court, she told me that the only way to clear the warrant was to turn myself in and show up to the court date. That is not what I wanted to hear. I was terrified. I'm going to jail, was my first thought. What happens if I go to jail? I thought. I don't have any money. I can't go to court without money. What am I going to do Lord? He said, Go. You will not be arrested. Trust me. Just go to the court date. I'll be with you.

When my court date came, I was sweating bullets. I was nervous and jittery. I just knew that the judge would make me pay my fines and court fees in full. And I had a lot of tickets. I knew I wouldn't be able to pay them in full, so I thought, "they are definitely going to arrest me." On the morning I was scheduled to appear in court, I sat eating my breakfast. I thought back to the moment I got the letter in the mail from the court, and I stuffed it in my drawer. I ignored my responsibilities. And now look at me. I had no choice but to go to court or else I would lose out on a great job opportunity. Clearly, I was not in control of my life like I thought I was. As I sat at the table eating my toast everything inside of me was saying, go back to bed and forget the whole thing. Forget that job, I thought. How can you work if they arrest you and you end up in jail? My anxiety was taking over. Through the chaos that was swarming around in my head, the Holy spirit spoke to me. Go to court. Trust me. I will be with you. I was so overwhelmed I couldn't do anything but pray.

Journal entry

February 2019

Lord, this morning I have very little faith about this court situation. I am trying to stay faithful and trust in your word, but it is extremely hard. I won't give up on you. You did not bring me this far to leave me. I will continue to trust your process, Lord. The job is still mine. I know that you have already worked this situation out. Devil you can't have my joy. Lord, I pray that whatever happens that you give me the strength to deal with it. Help me to accept the consequences of my actions. I will not worry Lord. I will trust in you. In Jesus name, I pray Amen.

Ironically, I drove myself to court that day. Ha! This is a judgement free zone. I was still paranoid from getting arrested. When I got there, I parked across the street from the court. I was scared that somebody from the court would see me driving up and penalize me. In retrospect, I can laugh because I was doing some serious overthinking. But in the moment I was terrified.

On my way into the courthouse something told me to turn around and go back home. But I ignored it. I stood on God's promise to me. The waiting process was tedious especially since I couldn't take my phone into court with me. When it was my turn to approach the judge, I was shaking like a leaf on a tree. My palms were sweaty. I could barely answer the judge's questions without stuttering. But I kept telling myself that God is with me. I'm good, he got me, I thought. Is it just me or are the judges in traffic court mean for no apparent reason? After asking me a bunch of questions and spitting a few nasty remarks at me. The judge told me to report back in two weeks for sentencing. I could've passed out. But I was so eager to leave the courtroom that after she dismissed me, I left as fast as I could.

I'm not sure if she told me to report back for sentencing to scare me. But when I appeared for my second court date, I was given a hefty fine (more than I expected) and sent on my way. As I approached the cashier's desk, I was told that I could make payment arrangements for my tickets and court fees. Beforehand, I thought that I would have to pay the court fees in full. And if I were unable to do so I thought that I would be arrested. That wasn't true. Once my payment arrangement was set up the clerk told me that my warrant would be lifted. I was so happy. I could have kissed that clerk. God showed up and rescued me, yet again.

I was so eager to call the recruiter and let her know that everything was taken care of. And that I would be able to start the job. She was excited to hear that I had worked everything out. She assured me that my start date would be pushed back. Meaning that I would start the job after the date originally given to me. I was so ecstatic that I did not care. I was just grateful that I still had a job.

Journal entry

February 2019

Dear God, I am so thankful that everything worked out at court today. I thank you for giving me the courage to show up. And the faith to believe in you. I am so glad that the situation is over. I will continue to believe in you and the plan that you have for my life. Guide me into the right direction. Please cover me. I thank the recruiter for working with me and giving me a chance to fix the mess that I created. I am so anxious to start this job. I cannot thank you enough Jesus. One thing I have learned through this situation is do not let the enemy enter my heart through disappointment. Thank you again Lord, so much. I love you. Amen

I realized that the situation had a more meaningful purpose. God wanted me to understand the bigger picture. Do you trust me enough to know that I will make a way regardless of your circumstance? The entire court situation terrified me. I did not want to go to jail. But I had enough faith to know that if I went that God would protect me. My situation reminded me of a story in the Bible. The story of Shadrach, Meshach, and Abednego and the blazing furnace (Daniel chapter 3). Their faith was so powerful and unwavering. I was not sure what the outcome of me showing up to court would be.

If I would be arrested or if they would let me walk free. But I was reminded of a scripture from Daniel 3:17, 'If we are thrown into the blazing furnace, the God we serve is able to deliver us from it." I told myself that no matter the outcome of my circumstance I would trust God. The Lord was testing my faith and my obedience. It had nothing to do with what was physically going on around me. Because God had already worked the situation out in my favor. It had more to do with my heart posture. And my faith.

Let me encourage you

Just because you have a relationship with God does not exempt you from life's struggles. Before I understood how being in relationship with God works, I thought followers of Christ didn't have to experience hardship. Being in relationship with God doesn't stop life from happening. Everybody will experience trials and tribulations no matter who they are. But as a person in relationship with God, I learned to trust him no matter what the circumstances looked like. Faith takes time to build. Your faith won't grow overnight. And my circumstances (being arrested, sacrificing, and showing up to court) may seem like small faith to some. But small faith is exactly what it takes to build big faith. Trusting God wasn't always easy for me. You must trust him through the tears and frustration. Sometimes trusting God is saying I don't know what is about to happen Lord, but I trust you. Sometimes trusting him is saying, I don't want to trust you because I am hurting but I am choosing to trust you anyway. Trusting God strengthened my faith. The more I was tested the stronger my faith became. The stronger my faith became the more I wanted to learn about God.

Christian Journey

Things were going well for me. It had been a couple of weeks since I started my new job and I loved it. The work was manageable. My coworkers were friendly. My relationship with God was thriving. And I was even considering baptism. However, although I had a great job, there was still no sense of fulfillment. I didn't feel like a career in nursing was my calling in life. Yes. It was a job. But I felt like I had more to offer the world. I knew I wasn't placed on this earth to be a nurse aide for the rest of my life. I wanted to know my purpose in life. What did God place me on this earth to do?

Journal Entry

March 2019

Dear Jesus, I need you to help me find my purpose. What is my passion? What is my calling? I know that I want to make good money. And I see myself in a field that requires me to be of service to others. But that's it. I need your help, Lord. I do not want to become overwhelmed. I want to be able to choose a calling/career that is perfect for me. I trust you.

I love you.

In Jesus' name, I pray.

Amen.

    I remember God speaking to me and his exact words were, I need you to get closer to me and build a stronger relationship with me before I give you any further instructions. I was a little frustrated, but I was still obedient. The Lord was always teaching me patience. His timing is always the best timing. So, while I waited for God to reveal my purpose. I followed his instructions and decided to strengthen our relationship. I continued spending time in his presence. I made sure that I consistently attended church service every weekend. I even joined a weekly Bible study that the church held, to grow closer to God. Our relationship was stronger than ever. And I felt like it was time for me to join a church home and be rebaptized. I contemplated it at first. And the devil tried to make me feel like I wasn't good enough. I knew the truth, but I still felt unworthy.

I was embarrassed by my past. I didn't believe that God would accept someone like me. I wasn't the ideal woman according to the Bible. I had sex out of wedlock. I was a gossiper. I had even given up on God in the past. How could I give my life to him considering my past? Negative thoughts always swarmed my head. God won't forgive you. What would people say if they saw someone like you giving your life to Christ? It's funny because thought I had to have the Bible memorized to be baptized. I thought I had to know every scripture. I was in a relationship with God. But I thought, for me to take that next step, for God to accept me, I had to be perfect.

After speaking with some of the elders in the church. I realized that no one is perfect. God welcomes us just as we are. Being a Christian is a lifelong process. There is no perfect time to give your life to Christ. Whenever I would be in church and my pastor would do the altar call. He would say: if you are looking for the perfect time to give your life to Christ, that time is now. My issue with getting baptized came from me being embarrassed of my past. I thought my sins were too sinful to be forgiven. But I had to realize that this is the very reason that God died on the cross: so that we can be forgiven for our sins. No matter how bad we think they are.

I figured out that I needed to ask God for forgiveness of my past sins. And then I needed to forgive myself. Asking God to forgive me was a lot easier than forgiving myself. Forgiving myself required me to face my past. I had to come face to face with all the sins I committed. But repentance was the only thing that would set me free.

Journal entry

April 2019

Dear Jesus, today I am excited for my baptism. I am excited for my transformation. I am so nervous to get to the church and start the process.

I pray that I enjoy today's service. Jesus, I thank you for this day. I am grateful for the wisdom that you have instilled in me. I thank you for changing my life. Thank you for giving me that push and the courage that I needed to transform. I would not be where I am today without your love, kindness, and patience. Thank you, Lord, for everything, I love you.

Today will be a good day in Jesus' name I pray.

Amen.

I was baptized April 6th, 2019. I was beyond nervous. My family came for support. Everything was perfect. It was one of the happiest moments of my life. For some reason during my alone season, I kept waiting for the point in my journey with God that things would get easier. But that moment never came. As I stated earlier the journey never gets easier. But my perspective changed. For example, God will give you the desire to live right. But that does not mean that your urge to sin will disappear. That is not how God works. He gives us free will.

If you pray and ask to be led by the Holy Spirit, he will place the desire on the inside of you. But it's up to you to wake up every day and make decisions based on your spirit and not your flesh. After being baptized I was under a tremendous amount of pressure. It became even harder for me to obey God. My desires and urges to sin were stronger than ever. I felt like I was moving backwards. I thought, shouldn't this walk with God be getting easier? I got closer to God and my life became harder. I was starting to regret making this change.

Journal Entry

April 2019

I thank you God for all that you have done for me. Lord, today I want to continue spending time talking with you. It's like some days I can hear your voice clearly. And other days I cannot decipher between my voice and yours. It's getting harder trying to be more like Christ. I never imagined that it would be easy. But I did not think that it would be this hard either. Oftentimes, I think about going back to my old habits. Back to the sin. It was more convenient, and I was under less pressure. Lord, I think about forgetting this relationship with you all the time. But fear stops me. The fear of living a life without you frightens me. I know that this relationship with you didn't happen out of coincidence. I am right where I need to be in life. I am supposed to be on this journey with you, Lord. I do not want to feel like this was all a mistake. Lord help me not be afraid. Help my unbelief. Give me the desire to be more like you Jesus.

After being baptized, I was trying hard to stay on track and be obedient to God. When I wasn't praying for strength, or fighting temptation, I was begging God to reveal my purpose. I started with asking myself what am I good at doing? The first thing that came to mind was cosmetology. I was good at styling my own hair. I figured if I was in search of my purpose why not start with a gift that has already been given to me. This was me taking matters into my own hands. Because God had already told me to be patient. I started to look up cosmetology schools. I even thought about investing in some master classes on social media. I prayed about my gift. I made up my mind that my calling was to be a hairstylist. I was literally all over the place. Seriously.

Journal Entry

April 2019

Dear God, I want to pray over my gift. You have given me this talent to do hair. If this is your will over my life then let it all manifest in your timing. I thank you for this gift and I pray that I can invest in my talent. Help me to believe in myself the way that you believe in me. Give me patience and obedience and help to turn my talent into a career for myself.

In Jesus name, I pray

Amen.

But God had other plans. And he was patient with me despite my disobedience.

God:

Just because you are good at something does not mean that it should become your purpose in life. Stop being impatient. Stop trying to take matters into your own hands. The fact that you are good at styling hair does not mean that it should be a career. It's a talent that was given to you, but it is not your life purpose. You will encourage others through your story. But right now, you are not ready. I am not done with you yet. There are still some tough situations that you will have to deal with. Be strong my love. Your time is coming.

Anytime God spoke to me, I wrote it down in my prayer journal. I wanted to be able to come back to his promises and his instructions. But I was confused and in disbelief by his message. I thought: You want me to encourage others through my story, how? What story do I have to tell? What tough situations will I have to deal with? Why was he telling me to be strong? I didn't try to figure out the meaning of God's message. I figured at the right time it would all make sense.

One day while scrolling social media, I came across an influencer who was a follower of Christ. I had been following her page on Instagram for a while and I was familiar with her inspiring story. Her name was Sherelle Marie. She was starting a 6-week mentoring program through her company called She Rose Detroit. The purpose of the program (to name a few things) was to help women grow in their relationship with Christ, strengthen their prayer life, and identify their God given gift. Sherelle was someone I trusted. So, once I learned more about the mentoring program, I was eager to apply for a spot. I needed more Godly council. I needed to be around Christian women who I could relate to. Sherelle was such a sweet and genuine person.

The mentoring program consisted of a small group of women. We studied the bible. We did weekly check-ins where Sherelle would call everyone individually and we would discuss what we had learned and have prayer. We started to create a sisterhood. The program was refreshing and just what I needed. She held us accountable. We were able to be completely honest with each other and Sherelle. She was such a God-fearing woman and what I loved most about her council was that she never gave advice based on her knowledge. She always led us back to God's word. I experienced my first fast during the program.

My first day of fasting was May 27th, 2019. I was so excited because I had never fasted before. We were fasting from food and social media. But I was also fasting so God could reveal my purpose. I was eager to see what he was getting ready to do in my life. The fast was a challenge. I knew I couldn't get through it in my own strength. Especially because I love food. But I prayed. And I read God's word consistently. I definitely had to lean on him for strength and support.

Journal Entry

May 2019

Today is my first day of fasting Lord and I am praying for strength and energy. I need you to be the source of my strength, God. Please be with me. I just want to be obedient to you and do your will. I want to be able to sit in your presence. I want to grow closer to you. I want to receive everything that you have for me. I ask that you remove the scales from my eyes. Open my ears and open my heart so that I can digest and meditate on your words. Protect my body during this process, Lord. My flesh is telling me that I cannot do this, but my spirit is telling me to lean not on my own understanding. Be with me God. I love you and I thank you.

In Jesus' name, I pray.

Amen.

I completed my first two days of the fast, but oday 3, I wasn't as successful. It was a Wednesday May 29th, 2019 I'll never forget it. I was doing well for the first half of the day. When fasting from food usually you rely on God's word in times of hunger, instead of actual food. Our fast was from 6am to 6pm. Instead of eating my usual breakfast that morning I turned down my plate and watched an online sermon instead.

When lunchtime rolled around, I felt a headache coming on. I received my usual text from Shamara asking me where we were going for lunch that day. At first, I was going to tell her that I was fasting because I knew that she would understand. But I decided against it. She suggested that we have lunch at the Chick-fil-a in the building where we both worked. I told her that I wasn't hungry but that I would meet her there anyway. We would have lunch together every day even if one of us wasn't hungry or had already eaten. I would be so happy to meet up with my sister on my lunch break because anytime we got together it was a good time. We would laugh and joke the entire time. Everything was a joke to us. From random people walking past, to old memories from our childhood. I ended up ordering my usual from Chick-fil-a a spicy chicken sandwich meal with a vanilla shake. We sat in the food court and talked through our 1-hour break.

Once our break was over, Shamara walked me back to my department like she always did after we would have lunch together. When it was time for us to go back to work, we would stop in the middle of the hallway and prolong our conversation. She would always say "See you later, text me". This particular time after saying our goodbyes, as she turned and walked away, I watched her. I watched her until she got to the end of the hallway and turned the corner. I have no idea why I did that. But after watching her leave I returned to work. That was the last time that I would ever see Shamara again, alive. I never imagined that would be our last time cracking jokes. That goodbye didn't feel like forever. It felt more like a see you later. You never know when it's your last time seeing a person. Nothing felt weird about that day. Nothing felt weird about the last moments that we shared. It felt like a normal day. Who knew May 29th, 2019, would be the day we shared our last meal together? I don't feel bad about breaking my fast. Honestly, I would feel bad if I hadn't.

Let me encourage you

Can I be honest with you? No one is filled with the Holy Spirit 24/7. Don't let anybody fool you. Following God is a challenge. It's about choices. You must be intentional for your relationship with Jesus to work. For your faith to work. You must wake up and choose to live by God's rules. You must choose to pray instead of worry. You must make a choice to be led by the Holy Spirit instead of your flesh. I don't always feel like praising God. But I choose to praise him anyway. Regardless of how I feel.

Following God is not for the weak. Respectfully. But it's the price that you pay for the promises that he has for you. If you are looking for someone to hold your hand, or you expect to experience a journey that's smooth sailing. Then following God is not for you. This journey requires work. But it's worth it. Life doesn't stop being life because you follow God. Your perspective changes.

Sometimes I have moments when I become overwhelmed. I get tired of waking up every day and spending time with God. Some days I just don't feel like it. I get tired of fighting the enemy. I asked God one day, "you want me to do this every day?" You want me to go to war with the enemy every day? I have to speak life into myself every day? I should tame my tongue every day? Even when that same smart mouth coworker keeps talking crazy, you want me to watch what I say to her EVERY DAY? This is too much. I don't get to take a break. Do I get any days off? The answer is NO! Satan is always out to attack. He never takes time off. He's coming to war whether you're prepared or not. I've noticed that whenever I've been neglecting my time with God, I feel like the devil comes at me ten times harder. He is very strategic. The Bible says in Ephesians 6:11 "Put on the full armor of God, so that you can take your stand against the devil's schemes. 1 Peter 5:8 says, "Be alert and of sober mind. Your enemy the devil prowls around like a roaring lion looking for someone to devour."

These scriptures remind us that the devil is always ready for war. We should always be alert and on guard. Spending time in God's word is just the preparation we need. Through the word, you learn to pray more and worry less. You learn to use scriptures to speak against the plans and tricks of the enemy. Every day will be a battle. Why would you take a break from God & risk showing up to the fight unprepared?

It's like a soldier going to war without his weapons. Or a boxer showing up to a fight without the proper training. The word is our weapon. It is our "proper training". We must stay in God's word so that we can remain focused. So that our faith can become stronger. We must stay in God's word so that we can speak life into ourselves whenever the enemy tries to control our thoughts. The devil is always trying to get you out of alignment with God. He is always looking for a way to sabotage the relationship between you and Christ. No matter how you feel you must be prepared to go to war with the enemy every day because he is always ready. Unfortunately, I learned this lesson the hard way.

Gracefully Broken

"Losing Booby"

Text message

FRI May 31, 2019 5:55pm

 Wyd?

SAT June 1, 2019 9:20am

(Looking eyes emoji) (confused emoji) (worried emoji)

June 1, 2019

    I woke up and checked my phone like I usually did. I texted Shamara the day before and she still had not texted me back. So, I sent her another text. It had been over 24 hours since I last talked to her and we never went this long without talking. I was worried, but I am an overthinker who tends to jump to conclusions quickly, so I told myself not to panic.

    I got on Facebook to ease my mind and wait for booby to return my message. As soon as I opened the app, I saw that I had a message from one of my sister's coworkers telling me to call her. My heart dropped to the pit of my stomach. I could not pinpoint exactly why she wanted me to call her, but I knew it had to be about Shamara. But again, I told myself not to get worked up as I proceeded to dial the lady's number.

    The first thing she asked me when she picked up the phone was had I talked to my sister. I am thinking to myself: what? why? She says, "she was scheduled to work today, and she hasn't showed up." Immediately my heart began to race. I felt short of breath. I knew something was wrong. Booby never misses a day of work. I hung up the phone and instantly got dressed. I had to go check on Booby to see if she was okay. I am rushing to get dressed, throwing on the first thing that I could find and blowing up Shamara's phone simultaneously. No answer. I called back. Still no answer. By this time, my younger sister comes out of her room and she is wondering why I am so anxious. I tell her what is going on and she says, "I am going with you." Thinking back, I wish I would have said, "No you can't go." But I had no idea what we were about to experience.

The entire ride to booby's house was turmoil. I was apprehensive, I wanted to think positive thoughts, but something kept telling me that she was not okay. I had a million scenarios playing in my head. And just when I started to calm my nerves the negative thoughts started to rush in again like a tidal wave. I thought, she has never not shown up for work. Oh my God, what if she is dead? The thought of that cut so deep that tears started to form in my eyes. My eyes started to sting, and a huge lump began to form in my throat. I did not want to believe that, so I said a prayer. That ride to her house felt like the longest ride of my life. I turned to my younger sister to see a tear sliding down her cheek. I could tell that she was afraid too, but we were both trying to be optimistic. I grabbed her hand and said, "it's gonna be okay." I spoke the words out loud to my little sister, but I was really trying to convince myself.

We pulled up to Booby's apartment complex. Immediately we jumped out of the car and ran up to the building. All I had was a head full of questions, eyes full of tears and some car keys but I was ready for whatever we were getting ready to walk into, or so I thought. I didn't have a key to her apartment, but I knew she was in there because I could see her car parked in her usual parking spot. That really made me panic. "Damn did she oversleep", I thought. What is going on? So, we rushed to the leasing office to see if they would let us in her building. I could barely hold back my tears at this point. I went in anxiously explaining the situation. Eyes running like a broken faucet, stumbling over my own words, I was an emotional wreck. For some reason, I was thinking that the woman in the leasing office would give me a key and I could just go into the apartment. She looked at me with the most unconcern facial expression I had ever seen. And she nonchalantly said, "I'm sorry ma'am but you'll have to call 911 and have them do a wellness check." I was enraged. Those words sent me over the edge. My perception was that she was dismissing my feelings. Here I am crying, frantic, snot running down my nose, heart pounding loud enough for the entire complex to hear. And this bitch is now adding fuel to the fire. I can look back now and respect the fact that she was doing her job but oh in that moment, I was pissed.

I left that leasing office crying hysterically. I was two seconds away from having a panic attack. My chest began to rise and fall rapidly, I'm sure I wasn't getting enough oxygen because my head started aching like I had been hit in the head with a brick, and it was almost impossible for me to catch my breath.

This was my dawg, my soulmate, and at that moment, I did not know if she was dead or alive. I refused to believe that she was hurt so I kept telling myself that she was exhausted from work the night before and that she had fallen into a deep sleep. "She is not hurt, she is okay." I kept telling myself. So, I did not call the police right away, instead I took matters into my own hands.

Shamara was a deep sleeper so it was not unlikely that she was just asleep. My younger sister and I went around to the back of the complex to Booby's balcony which happened to be slightly open. Seeing that slightly opened balcony made us both weary, but we are more so concerned about Booby.

My adrenaline is pumping at this point. I was desperate and willing to do whatever it took to get us into her apartment -that included breaking in. My frantic mind was thinking, if I lift my baby sister up on to the balcony she could get into the apartment and check on booby. That plan failed tremendously. I don't know if I was too anxious to focus or if it was God intervening on what could have been a horrific outcome. I tried with all my might to lift my baby sister's 130-pound body up onto that balcony. But she did not have the upper body strength to pull herself up. I was frustrated by this point. Angry at Booby for not answering her phone, angry at my little sister for not being strong enough to lift herself up onto the balcony. I was just livid.

We went back around to the front of the building to see if we could catch someone coming out so that we could go in. While we waited, I rang her buzzer multiple times. Still no answer. Finally, a guy let us in. I still didn't have a key, but I was one step closer to seeing my sister. We beat on her apartment door for what seemed like forever- I am sure we woke her neighbors. After a while, I decided to call the police. I kept thinking maybe her phone is on do not disturb. Maybe she fell asleep with the phone under her pillow. I called time after time & still no answer but that didn't stop me from calling. It literally took the police like 7 minutes to arrive. But I was so stressed out that those seven minutes felt like hours. They arrived calm and asking a slew of questions. With my anxiety through the roof, I explained what was going on. The entire time I'm thinking, please officer just open the door so that we can see her. I need to know that she is alright.

"How old is she?" "Does she drink alcohol?" "Does she have any health issues?" The officer asked.

Right before they opened the door to her apartment one officer turned to us and said, "You wait here we'll go inside and make sure everything is ok, once we know she's ok we'll let you come in."

My heart sank. I'm thinking: what? Why? I figured once they got there, they would just let us go in.

They went in calling her name. Shamara! Shamara! It's the police. Shamara! Are you ok? Shamara! Shamara! They knocked on her bedroom door. And continued calling her name. Shamara! Shamara! Suddenly it got quiet. We're all screaming: What's going on? Is she ok?" "Can we come in?" "Why is it taking so long?"He never answered our questions.

His reply was "we'll be out in a minute" The EMS showed up and my first thought was oh my god she's hurt. And then a guy shows up with a medical bag. I couldn't tell where he worked because he wasn't wearing a badge, but I do remember him going into her apartment. It still never crossed my mind that booby was hurt. I guess I was so busy praying for the best I wasn't expecting the worst.

After another round of us shouting questions from the hallway to Shamara's bedroom, the officers finally came out to speak to us. It was something about the cops' body language. I could sense his uneasiness. He slightly dropped his head and said, "She is deceased." I couldn't believe what I had just heard. "What happened?" I said. "We're not sure but it looks like she died in her sleep. Her phone is on the charger, her watch and tablet are plugged in. We looked around her place and everything appears to be intact. Her glasses are in the case – there is no force of entry or no suspect of foul play."

I'll never forget the look on my little sister's face. I wanted to scream, cry, punch holes in the wall, and fight but I couldn't. My first reaction was no reaction at all. No emotions. No tears. Nothing. I was in complete shock. I had my little sister sitting right in front of me watching my every move. I'm the big sister. I couldn't let her see me breaking down. I had to be strong for the both of us. So, I held it all in. I just held my little sister while she cried.

As I was holding my little sister tightly, rocking her back and forth. Overwhelmed with emotions I took a deep breath, and my next words were "okay so what do we do next?"

The officers proceeded to tell us our next steps but everything sounded muffled. Until they asked us if we wanted to go in and see her. My brain was screaming, "Go see for yourself!", "Maybe they're wrong". "Maybe Booby is alive". I stood in her doorway, but my feet wouldn't move. I was terrified. Traumatized by everything that had just taken place. I didn't want to see my best friend like that. Lifeless. Cold. I wanted to go in and see if it was really her, but I couldn't bring myself to do it. Is she really gone? What happened? None of this makes sense. Did somebody hurt her? Did she suffer? How long had she been dead in the house? It's my fault I left her here. She would have never left me alone like this if the tables were turned. I should have called her Thursday night after we finished texting. I should have come over yesterday morning when she didn't reply to my text.

My thoughts were interrupted by a woman with a camera in her hand. She was coming out of Booby's apartment asking me a million questions. She told me that somebody had to identify her body before the coroner's office removed it from the home. I felt another lump forming in my throat. I thought, I am going to pass out if I have to do this. I was screaming on the inside: please lady, don't make me do this. PLEASE I've been through enough for one day. I don't know how much more I can take. Please have some sympathy for me ma'am I can't identify her I just can't.

I was answering questions. Consoling my baby sister. And on top of everything my momma was calling. I hadn't even had time to process what had just happened. And now I had to gather up the strength I had left to identify my best friend's body. I wish it could have been anybody but me. My stomach was in knots. I felt lightheaded. I thought, "I've experienced enough trauma to last me a lifetime, let alone one day." My heart was racing. I just knew I would collapse. My heart literally couldn't take it anymore. I kept thinking: "What if she doesn't look like herself?" How am I getting ready to do this? Is this even real? Is this really happening right now? The woman turned her camera toward me and scrolled through 3 pictures. Each time she stopped on a picture my heart broke a little more. All I could do was nod my head. I was furious with this woman. I just wanted her to make it stop. It already felt like somebody had stuck a knife into my chest. And with each picture it felt like the knife was being driven deeper and deeper. This was really Booby that I was identifying. I couldn't believe it.

I was so glad when that was over. Shamara looked peaceful. Like she was asleep. I still didn't want to see her like that. But I couldn't be mad at the lady for doing her job.

After that was over. I told myself that I needed to go outside. I needed some fresh air. How was I going to tell my momma that her baby was gone? How do you even explain that to a mother? Once outside I realized that I hadn't told anybody the news yet. Nobody knew but myself, Kyra, and Booby's coworker who lived in the apartment building. I was panicking. My momma wasn't even in town when it happened. She took my brother to his college orientation in Ohio. I couldn't give her the horrible news over the phone. I have to wait until she gets home to tell her, I thought. I had so much pressure on me. I didn't know where to start first or what to do. At that moment, I just needed someone to lean on. Someone to hold me while I cried and screamed. But I couldn't break. As bad as I wanted to, I couldn't. "Not right now. Not at this moment." I thought.

I took a deep breath. I proceeded to stand on the sidewalk to try to wrap my head around it all. I don't remember what happened in the moments leading up to this one but the next thing I know, I heard my little sister say, "Here look this way." She proceeded to distract me. She tried grabbing me by my arm and turning me in the opposite direction of the apartment entrance. I was wondering what in the world she was doing. I disregarded everything she said and focused my attention on the complex entrance. There I saw the coroners carrying a body bag. It was a gray bag with black handles. I froze. That image is forever engraved into my memory.

The sight of that completely broke me. I felt my soul leave my body. I felt lifeless. I thought I had nothing left to give after what I had just experienced. And the sight of her body being carried sucked the life out of me. I wanted to scream, "she can't breathe in that bag! Get her out of there!" But nothing came out. I was in total shock. I had never felt anything like that in my life. It all seemed like a nightmare. A nightmare that I wished so badly that I could wake up from. And then I thought, "booby probably never thought that when she walked into her apartment it would be her last time." Please don't drop her", I thought. "Unzip the bag a little so that she can breathe at least," I thought. My mind was all over the place. At this point I was damn near delusional.

I was stuck in my tracks. A million things running through my head. Shamara's co-worker- who was with us at the time- snapped me out of my thoughts by suggesting that we sit in her car for a while. I got in, looked at my phone and I had a missed call from my auntie "Damn. I still haven't told anyone yet," I thought. Maybe I should tell Shamara's job first because she never showed up and they may start to suspect something.So, I called her supervisor. I dialed her job number and as the phone rang, I grew nervous. I had no idea what to say. I have never in my life had to tell someone that a person died. Let alone a person that I was close to.

Me: Hey this is LaKrystal

Shamara's supervisor: Hey LaKrystal so what can you tell us?

I opened my mouth and the only thing that came out was, "Shamara died today."

Shamara's supervisor took a huge *gasp* And then she said, "I am so sorry LaKrystal, what happened?"

I honestly had no idea what happen. But I told her the only thing that I knew at the time. "She passed away in her sleep", I said.

After that our conversation everything else became a blur. Just hearing myself say those words crushed my spirit even more. It just didn't make sense.

My cousin Chass was close to Shamara. She was one of the first people I texted when I couldn't get a hold of her. Between her and my momma my phone had been ringing non-stop since we got to Booby's apartment.

But I couldn't tell them anything at the time because I didn't have any information. Before I could return Chass' call, she called me. I had no idea what to even say. But I had to tell her. I repeated the same sentence that I had just told Booby's supervisor. "Shamara died". I just remember my cousin screaming into the phone. Each time I revealed the news to someone else it became even more devastating. But I was emotionless. I was calm. I had nothing left to feel. I was in denial. As well as in a state of shock. I couldn't even believe my own words and they came from my mouth. I didn't want to tell anybody else. But I had to tell my momma. But how? She was three hours away from us. I couldn't let someone else tell her. I wanted her to hear it from me. I started to walk toward the back of the apartment building. I called her phone and before I could say anything she picked up the phone and said, "What's wrong?" She knew something had to be wrong because we were ignoring her calls.

"Ummmm" I stuttered.

"WHAT'S WRONG?" she said. Her voice now ten times louder than before.

"Shamara died today," I said in a low, calm voice. I could hear her let out a loud gasp. But all I could say is "it's ok ma try to calm down." I began to pace back and forth at this point. I wanted to cry, but nothing came out.

As soon as I told my momma and my cousin more calls started to come in. I had just witnessed the most traumatic experience of my life. And now I had to relieve each moment by explaining what happened every time someone called my phone. "I just want this day to be over," I thought, "I just need some peace and quiet."

Journal Entry

6/1/2019

Lord, I don't know what this is about, but I am not okay.

I will never be the same. My family will never be the same.

We lost a good person today. I don't understand this.

I don't want to wake up tomorrow. But I have to be strong for my family.

Please, Lord, give me strength. Give my family the strength to make funeral arrangements.

Please protect us, Lord. We cannot do this alone. We all need you.

Help me understand why?

I can't believe this.

Let me Encourage you.

Life is short. I must have heard that phrase a hundred times growing up. People use this phrase all the time and we often repeat it without even understanding it's true concept. I don't believe a person is truly able to grasp the concept of something unless they go through it. Unless they are personally affected. I've had plenty of people tell me how horrible it was suffering with COVID. But I could never truly relate because I never had the virus. I've had mothers of all ages tell me how painful childbirth is and the stories sound devastating. But I can only go off what I've heard. Until I bear children of my own, I could never understand what mothers go through. Sympathizing with a person does not automatically give you the ability to understand what they have been through. You could say that you understand but you really don't. Trust me once you've experienced something first-hand it takes on a whole new meaning.

    Grieving changed my entire life. Losing Shamara showed me just how short life is. Cherish the moments that you have with the people that you love. I mean it, sincerely. And I know it's a cliché. But take it from me. It's the truth. I was laughing while eating lunch with Booby May 29th. 2019 and three days later she was gone.

I could have never seen that one coming. Now I can say: "Don't take your loved ones for granted". Which is another cliché. But I won't. Because I don't think it's the people that we take for granted. It's time. We take time for granted. Not purposely. Time feels like forever. Be honest. Doesn't it feel like we have time to do anything and everything? But that's not true.

We unconsciously say stuff like "Oh I got time", or "I'll do it tomorrow". But what if tomorrow never comes? My sister had so many things planned that she wasn't able to do. She had so many goals set that she will never get a chance to accomplish. She was saving for a vacation that she never got the chance to experience. She made plans to go back to school to obtain her nursing degree. Can you imagine making plans today and not being around next week to see your plans through? In no way am I trying to instill fear in you. My message to you is to live your life to its full potential.

If there is something that you've been wanting to do, please, do it! Take the trip to Bora Bora. Buy the new car. And always remember to tell your loved ones just how much you love and appreciate them.

We have no way of knowing when our time is up on this Earth. But each day we are closer to the date. Life is too unpredictable to be doing anything that doesn't bring you joy. Whether that's staying in a relationship, working a specific job, or being afraid to walk in your purpose. Do what makes you happy. Live life knowing that you went after everything that you wanted. Be satisfied knowing that you did exactly what your heart desired.

Losing myself

"You're so strong".

The mere thought of those words makes me cringe. I hated when people would say that to me because I didn't feel strong. I was a mess. I would hold it together during the day and cry myself to sleep at night. I was numb. Numb to all the hurt and pain. I didn't get a chance to express my emotions in the moment like everybody else had. From the moment I found out that my sister was dead, I suppressed my emotions. My younger sister was with me when I received the news. She was watching my every move. I didn't feel like I could cry and fall apart like I wanted to at that moment. I needed to be strong for my baby sister. I didn't have time to be sad or angry or even process what had just happened. Instead, I had to identify the cold, and stiff body of my best friend. I had to watch someone I grew up with be carried from her home. Not to mention the worst part of all, I had to tell my mother that she would never see her oldest daughter again.

Just when I thought it was safe for me to cry and take everything in, it was time to plan Shamara's funeral. I was exhausted. But I felt like it was my duty to make sure that everything was perfect for her homegoing service. I owed it to her. It took every ounce of strength that I had left to write out my sister's obituary. That was the weirdest, most heartbreaking thing that I have ever done. I thought we had more time together. I figured we would grow old, have a couple kids, and then our grandkids would bury us. The thought of me burying my dawg never crossed my mind. Summing up her 27 years of life didn't sit well with me. I've read so many obituaries of young people whose lives have been cut short. But when it's you on the other end of that pad and paper recollecting somebody's life, it hit different. I had no idea what to say. I was angry because she had barley lived her life. It just wasn't fair.

Everything felt spooky to me. From picking out the last outfit that she would wear to choosing the casket that she would be buried in. I felt like I was in a movie. Stuff just kept coming. My soul was tired. All I wanted to do was cry. All I wanted to do was rest. I just wanted a moment to process everything. The days leading up to her funeral were busy. There was always something that needed to be done. And the main thing that was running through my mind was "when do I get to exhale?". "When can I truly be alone with my thoughts?". So, no, from my perspective I wasn't strong. I was in a daze. Nothing seemed real. I suppressed the emotions that I wanted to express. There was no time to stop and grieve. I had to keep going.

Journal entry

June 2019

Lord, no disrespect, but I am so frustrated with you. My best friend is gone. You knew what she meant to me. You knew how much I loved her. I don't understand any of this. I really wish that this did not happen. I am sad, angry, confused, hurt, alone and lost. I miss Booby more than ever. What will I learn from all of this? Will I die next? I hate feeling like this. Just take my life now, Lord. I am sick of life and everybody in it. I am ready to isolate myself from the world. Fuck everybody. Fuck everything. My life will never be the same. I miss you Booby and if you can hear me, I wish I was with you.

I love you forever.

I couldn't control the fact that I was the one who went to her house that day. But I was furious. Why me?

Why did I have to be the person to identify her body? Why did I have to be the person to tell everybody that she was dead? Why did I have to help plan a funeral and write an obituary? WHY ME?

I was traumatized. And it felt like the task just kept coming. It was torture for me. I just needed a moment to myself. I was furious with everybody. Because although I was suffering, enduring one heavy burden after the next, everybody was being inconsiderate. Everybody wanted to express their opinion about what was being done. Shamara's casket was closed at her service. Everybody had an issue with that. A few people weren't mentioned in her obituary. People had an issue with that. I was fighting for my life trying my best to hold it together. And people were literally disregarding everything that I had been through. I couldn't close my eyes without seeing her dead body and people had the nerve to text me asking why her casket was going to be closed? I was crying myself to sleep at night and people were questioning why their name wasn't mentioned in her obituary? Ain't that bout a bitch. My life was a nightmare. But I couldn't waste my energy arguing with people or cursing them out. Especially since I barely had energy to complete the task for the funeral. As angry as I was, as hurt as I was, as tired as I was, I kept going.

Journal entry

June 2019

Today I feel tired. I am not ready to do anything. I am not ready to go anywhere. I do not want to be around anybody. I just wish I could sleep the day away. I am tired of this. Fuck life.

The next task on the list was to pack up her apartment. I couldn't catch a break. On the way there, I felt like I was having a mild heart attack. I have no idea what a mild heart attack feels like, but it felt like a child was sitting on my lungs. For a few seconds, I had a hard time catching my breath. It was starting to set in that Booby was gone. I thought: She's never coming back. I'm really on my way to clean out her apartment. Being in her room after everything that had happened was spooky. Especially without her being there. The thought of me standing in the same room that she took her last breath in didn't sit well with me. As I took the clothes from her drawers and placed them into laundry bags I tried to think of the good times. I tried hard not to cry. I thought about the times I would spend the night with her. We would make late night snack runs and come back to her house and stay up all night laughing and watching tv. I thought about how 5 months earlier we were all in her living room bringing in the new year together. I thought about all the times she asked me to come over and spend the night. I regret every time that I ever declined. I regret all the arguments that we had. I regret the times when I was mean to her for no reason at all. I regret not hugging her enough. Cleaning out her apartment was devastating. It was confirmation that she really was gone and never coming back.

My family and I received a lot of love and support during that difficult time. I am forever grateful for everybody that supported us. But it felt like once the funeral was over the love stopped. I'm not upset with anybody. And I'm not holding anything against anybody. I just realized how much you need that same love and support months and even years after the fact.

Don't get me wrong, I still have close family and friends who I know are always in my corner. But everybody was okay to go back to their normal lives after her funeral. My family and I couldn't go back to ours.

Journal entry

July 2019

Hey Boob, I miss you sooooooooooooo much. It's almost been 2 months since you've been gone. It feels so weird living without you. I keep asking God: what does all of this mean? I just wish that you could come back. I wish I could hear your voice or see your face. I have been suffering ever since you've been gone. And I don't know if it's because I don't know how to deal with your death or if I hate my own life so much that I'm giving up. I drink a lot more now even though before you left I wasn't drinking at all. I felt like I was starting to get my life on track. But now I feel defeated. I feel like I'm back at square one. This hurts like hell. I will never understand. I will never get over this. My best friend is gone and never coming back. I hate going to work. I hate doing anything that involves me getting off the couch and interrupting my drinking sessions. Guess what? I'll have my license back this weekend. And I paid off my school balance. I know you would be proud of me and have a joke or two. Please stay in my heart Booby, never leave. I miss your laugh. Your jokes. I miss us getting on each other's nerves. I miss sleeping over at your house. I miss our snack runs. Nobody could ever replace you. I miss you more than anything my dawg. I wish we could have one of our talks. There is so much other stuff that I want to tell you. Nobody laughs when I recite scenes from certain movies like you used to. It makes me sad that my person is gone. Only you understood me. My baby always and forever. I miss you my G. You would have been twenty-great (28) next month. I know you would have taken lots of pictures. And had a bunch of nice captions. How are we supposed to celebrate your birthday without you? Boob, I don't ever go this long without seeing you. And vice versa. It's crazy, man. I wish it was all a dream. You were the coolest, most down to earth, most loyal and kindhearted person I have ever met. Gone too soon. Forever 27. I know you hated that so much. That's why I said it. The worst part about all of this is that after your funeral everybody went back to their normal lives. But I couldn't. Because from that day forward I had a new normal. I had to learn to live without you. In the beginning, I felt so angry when life continued to go on after you died. It was selfish to me that we still had life and you didn't. I hated seeing people with their sister, best friend or person. Because I don't have mine. And it sucks. I feel like quitting my job soon. I am overwhelmed and I don't feel appreciated. Like I used to always tell you, "Protect your peace." I need to protect mine. My head is all over the place Booby. Believe it or not you kept me sane. Now I am lonely. I feel alone in this world even though I have good people around me. My baby boo. Come back to me please. Come visit me in my dreams. Help me get back on track because I can't do this life thing without you. This is unfair.

One day I was sitting on the floor in my room - my back against the bed. I was furious with God. I asked him: why? Why did you take my sister away from me? Why are you allowing me and my family to suffer? I was livid. I decided to get everything off my chest. I said: Jesus, how could you? I've done everything you've asked of me. Without hesitation. I was obedient. Even when things got challenging for me. I spent time with you day in and day out. I stop fornicating. I even got baptized and surrendered my life to you. And this is the thanks I get. You don't love me. You would not have allowed this to happen if you did. I trusted you. And where has it gotten me? Then I sat and cried. I wasn't expecting a response from God. I was just frustrated, and I needed him to know how I felt.

God spoke to me in a way that I have never heard him speak before. He said, "Shamara is my child. She never belonged to you. In fact, none of your loved ones belong to you. You don't even have ownership of yourself. You belong to me. You are all my children. I was gracious enough to allow you to spend 27 years with her. But now I need her back.Just as I will need you back one day." I did not want to hear anything God had to say. I was hurting. The message literally went in one ear and out of the other. Until he asked me a question that made me stop and think. He asked: is your faith conditional? The question caught me off guard. Conditional means subject to, implying, or dependent upon a condition. God was asking if my faith was dependent upon certain conditions. He said, ``Is it only okay for you to trust me when it's convenient for you? You can trust me when I am giving you everything that you ask for. You have faith in me when everything in your life seems easy. But what happens when your faith is tested on a different level? What happens when the pain seems like too much to bear?

Because Shamara was physically removed from your life is that a reason to stop believing in me? Is that a reason to stop having faith? Shouldn't your faith be unconditional? Are you able to trust me when the unthinkable happens or is your faith conditional?

At that moment I started to view the situation from a different perspective. I realized how selfish I sounded. Instead of blaming God for Booby's death and being angry with him for taking her away, I should be more appreciative. I should be grateful that I got to experience life with such a beautiful person. Was my faith conditional? When I was tested in my previous season the trials stretched me, but they never broke me. I was uncomfortable but never to the point where I questioned God or my faith. Losing Shamara broke me. I had nothing left to give. No faith. No fight. No energy. Nothing. I was taught when things get rough to go to God in prayer. But in this situation, I had no desire to pray. My faith wasn't conditional. It had never been tested to this magnitude. Even though I knew God had my best interest. And I needed to take into consideration the things that he told me. I did not want to hear him. Yes. God was right about everything. And I knew that.

But I was angry. So, my anger trumped my obedience.

I was upset with God. So upset that I went weeks without talking to him. I pushed my Bible to the back of my closet, and I refused to open it. There was no way that I would believe anything that the Lord had to say. He could not help me. I blamed him for what had happened. After months of walking with Christ I was done living by God's rules. I was going to do things my way. I started to live a lifestyle that I couldn't recognize. It wasn't that I stopped hearing from God. I just chose not to listen.

This season of my life was devastating. I felt like I was losing everything. My best friend. My faith. And my mind. The first few months after losing my sister were the hardest for me. The entire day (June 1st, 2019) was engraved in my memory. I was traumatized. I had a hard time sleeping. I would try to rest, and my brain would replay everything. I would close my eyes and see her deceased body. This kept me scared and anxious. My body would be tired, but I couldn't close my eyes without reliving that traumatic experience. One night I was so afraid that I didn't sleep at all. I kept my light on all night. Wrapped myself in my covers and sat in the middle of my bed until the sun came up. My mind wouldn't stop racing. And the flashbacks were too overwhelming. Some days I slept and some days I went without sleeping. The first 4 months after her death I slept with my light on. I was too afraid to sleep in the dark. It was as if being in the dark triggered me. Staying awake was easier than reliving what I went through.

My flashbacks weren't only at bedtime. On several occasions they would happen in the middle of the day. It confused me. Sometimes I was triggered by certain things that made me think about June 1st. And other times I didn't have to be triggered and I still thought about that day. I remember being outside one day. I don't remember where exactly. But I saw two construction workers carrying loads of two-by-four. They were working together. One man was on one side and one man was on the other side. I was triggered immediately. My mind went back to Shamara's apartment on June 1st. My brain didn't comprehend the fact that I was looking at two construction workers. Instead, my brain saw the corners carrying booby's body. A lump formed in my throat. My heart started beating rapidly and tears began to form in my eyes. I couldn't escape what had happened. I felt like it was haunting me. I was always being triggered by so many things. So many different things reminded me of Shamara. Seeing certain things would place me right back at her apartment on the day of her death. And I had no control over any of it. I was hurting. I was frustrated. I remember thinking to myself your best friend is dead. What do you have to live for? Why are you still here? You won't be able to live without Shamara. The devil would constantly get in my head and I accepted every thought that he presented to me. Not only was I grieving the loss of my sister, but, on top of that, my mind was forcing me to relive the moments that I wanted to forget. I was exhausted physically and mentally. I wanted my mind to stop racing and having flashbacks. I thought: death must be better than life. I felt like death was the only way to permanently stop my pain. I never had any suicide attempts, only thoughts of suicide. I thought about taking pills. I thought about crashing my car. I would even pray to God and ask him to let me die in my sleep. I didn't want to die. I honestly just wanted the pain to stop. I didn't succeed with suicide. So, I gave up on life. I wasn't living recklessly. But I didn't care about the decisions that I was making either. I didn't care what happened to me. I was in a dark space. I woke up on several different days and I would bawl my eyes out. Not just because I was hurting but because God kept allowing me to live another day. I didn't want to live anymore.

I didn't have the energy to do anything. Not even to work. I would lay in my bed and weep at the thought of going to work the next day.

The thought alone gave me anxiety. I would get tired just thinking about it. So, I would call in and stay home. This happened so much I'm surprised I didn't lose my job. I didn't have the energy to be around people. I would rather not put on a pretend smile. I tried to stay away from anything that required my energy. I isolated myself. I spent a lot of time in my room - either in my bed underneath the covers or laid across my bedroom floor. When I decided to leave my room, I went from my bed to the living room couch. It became my comfort zone. I sat on the couch so much that I'm sure I left a dent in the cushion. I would literally sit, drink and binge watch tv series. I would drink to suppress my emotions. Morning, afternoon, and night. Whenever I felt the urge. This wasn't the best solution because drinking made me emotional. I would cry even more when I drank then when I didn't drink. But that didn't matter to me. I drank sometimes just so I could go to sleep.

As stated previously trying to go to sleep was a hassle for me. But drinking relaxed me. Drinking didn't take away my pain. But if I drank enough, it helped me cope. I would purposely drink until I was tired. Or I would drink until I was discombobulated and all I could do is sleep.When I was intoxicated, I didn't have to worry about seeing Shamara's face whenever I close my eyes. Or having flashbacks of my best friend, who wasn't 30 years old yet, lying in a casket. Whenever I drank before bed, I got the rest that I had been missing. I knew that the constant drinking was not the way to deal with my pain. Logic wasn't a priority. When you're hurting you just want a way to ease or "get rid of the pain."

Grief, Then

Most people make it seem like grief is something that one can overcome. In my opinion, grief is perceived as a process that one should be capable of getting over. According to the American counseling association, grief is a natural reaction to loss or change. Grief is most commonly discussed in relation to the death of a loved one, however grief can be experienced following any major change. That may be true in certain circumstances. People may be able to get over the loss of a job. They may even be able to get over the loss of a relationship. But death hits differently. I can't overcome death. It's not something that you get over. Instead, I had to learn how to cope.

My first encounter with grief was frustrating. I didn't understand that it was a process. All I knew was that I was hurting, and that I wanted the pain to stop. I didn't think I would recover after losing my sister. Because the pain was just too much to handle. My family had a "new normal" that didn't consist of Shamara. How could we ever go back to living how we once had before?

I felt like I had been knocked flat on my face. I wanted to get up and keep fighting. But I could not. I did not have the ability to do so. Have you ever seen the movie Paid in Full directed by Charles Stone? There is a scene in the movie when the two characters (Ace and Rico) are having a conversation. In the scene, Ace has recently been shot. Rico says, "Aye niggas get shot everyday B, you'll be alright nigga." Ace replies to Rico and says, "My body is different, I'm breathing different." Trying to return to my normal life while grieving had me feeling like Ace. I would never compare grieving to being shot. But I understood where he was coming from. I'm not the same person that I was before this happened to me. Life feels different. Before Shamara died, I thought I knew who I was. But afterwards, I wasn't so sure. I didn't recognize myself anymore. I was using strength that I didn't know I had. "Who is this person?" I thought. How was I able to make it through such a traumatic experience? How was I able to keep my sanity? I've done things that I never imagined I could do. Where did this strength come from?

I felt like life was forcing me to continue living like nothing had happened. I was Ace (Paid in Full) and life was Rico. I kept hearing, you're strong. You'll be alright, God wouldn't put more on you than you can handle. But in my head I'm like: No, I'm not strong, I won't be okay. Life didn't even feel the same. I don't think people understood that my whole world had been flipped upside down.

Once I realized that there was no way to take away my pain. I started doing things that either numbed the pain or distracted me from it. I isolated myself. I tried going back to work to distract myself from the pain. I even tried dating to fill the void in my heart.

I had no desire to be around people socializing. I didn't want people talking to me asking questions. I deleted my social media accounts. I hated to see people going on with their lives. Because I felt like I couldn't go on with mine. I felt stuck. I couldn't go back in time, but I didn't want to move forward either. I did not want to live. I felt guilty about continuing to live life without Shamara. Being isolated made things a little easier for me. I didn't have to put forth any effort. Being home, in my room under the covers, brought me comfort. Being at home, sitting in my misery, was more convenient for me than facing the world. I knew that I wasn't ready to handle the outside world. Anytime that I found myself trying to return to my normal life I would randomly burst into tears. I was uncomfortable. It didn't take much for me to think about my sister. Especially when I would hear or see things that reminded me of her. Something so simple as a song on the radio could bring tears to my eyes. Or riding past a restaurant that we visited together. Even seeing the type of car that she used to drive brought tears to my eyes. Shamara was ALL that I knew. It's always been the two of us. Our friendship. Our sisterhood. It may sound weird but it's almost as if I had to unlearn how to operate in the relationship that we shared. Because it doesn't exist anymore. I became accustomed to spending time with her: picking up my phone and calling her whenever I needed to. Now that I can't do those things I'm frustrated. It's painful for me because my love for her has nowhere to go. Of course, I have other friendships. I've created a sisterhood with several different people. But it's not the same. It's impossible for me to give the love that I have for her, to anybody else.

Returning to my normal life meant heading back to work. Work was almost unbearable. It was pure torture for me. I thought it would be my escape. But it was a constant reminder of Shamara. We worked for the same company and we would always spend time with each other on our lunch breaks. There weren't too many places I could go at work that didn't remind me of her. A simple area like the food court would have me rushing to the nearest restroom so that I could privately cry in a stall. I felt like I was going crazy. I didn't understand what I was going through. Thank God, I had great co-workers. From day one they were supportive of me. When I would call into work, my supervisor was understanding. When I would be standing at the nurses' station ready to break down, I was given breaks so that I could pull myself together. I'll never forget being at work one day. I had just come back from my lunch break. This was a horrible day, so horrible that I was drinking on my lunch break. I got back to my work area and I was sitting at the nurse's station in a daze. I was so far from reality and my supervisor walked up to me and she said: "do you want to go home?" I nodded my head yes. I'm not sure if it was the look on my face or if she felt sorry for me but sending me home that day meant everything to me. I felt like I was slowly dying. It was as if I wasn't living anymore, just existing. It was like she walked up and read my mind. My Meyers Lab family (my coworkers) was the family that I didn't know I needed at the time. A few of them were there for me when I wasn't strong enough to be there for myself, whether it was them speaking life into me, being there to listen, or giving me resources (books and journals) to help me cope. I am forever grateful for them all. Even though I had the support from my work family, that didn't dismiss the fact that I was grieving; and using distractions to hide my pain.

Dating was a distraction that I used not only to hide my pain, but to fill a void. Dating allowed me to focus my attention on someone else and their life. According to Psychology Today, there are five stages of grief: Denial, Anger, Bargaining, Depression and Acceptance. I experienced each stage in no specific order. In fact, I went through a few of those stages more than once. But one stage that I went through that isn't listed above is the stage of trying to fill the void that was left in my heart after losing my sister.

Losing Shamara broke my spirit. I felt like there was a hole in my heart. I tried filling that hole with the love from someone else. I wanted my heart to feel whole again. I started dating 3 months after Booby's death. This wasn't a good idea because I could barely get out of the bed each morning. There was no way that I was capable of being in a relationship. I couldn't last five minutes at work without crying hysterically. Why was I trying to jump into a relationship? Because the heart wants what the heart wants. Mine just wanted to be restored.

I was grieving. My emotions where all over the place. But I wanted to be happy again. I wanted somebody to make me smile again. I wanted somebody to love me. I felt alone. I unconsciously gave the man that I was dating a huge responsibility. It was his job to make me happy again. It was his responsibility to be there for me. He had no idea that he was given this role in my life. I never told him, but I expected it from him. He came into my life and fulfilled my expectations. He brought joy back into my life. I missed smiling and laughing. My life hadn't been the same since booby died. After three months of suffering. I had something to look forward to. Someone had my back, and someone cared about me just like Shamara used to. He was giving me the time and the attention that I so desperately wanted. Although I was dating, and it helped to distract me for a while. I couldn't escape reality. As they say: life goes on. I had to continue living life even though I wasn't ready to; and that frustrated me. I felt like life was being insensitive. I felt like I was being forced to get over Shamara's death. You want me to go to work? I barely felt like showering. You want me to be in good spirits? Celebrate holidays and birthdays? Why? I had no energy to do any of those things. Deep down I was irritated with everything. I wanted the world to stop for a few months. I wanted life to stop and let me grieve.

My grieving process was unique. It almost felt like my brain was wired differently. It felt like a switch was flipped and I was a completely different person. I didn't comprehend things like I would have if I were not grieving. I didn't want people's sympathy. Mainly because their way of expressing it was by complimenting my strength. I think it was because they didn't know what else to say. If I had a dollar for every time somebody told me how strong I was, I could've paid off my student loans. I get it. The kind words were coming from a sincere place. But I did not want to hear any of it. During my grieving process I stayed in the "Anger" stage the longest. One of the things I hated to see was other people out with their sisters or best friends. If I couldn't have mine, I didn't want to see anybody with theirs. It sounds crazy but grieving will make you feel like that. When I would see people out with their sister, or best friend, I grew envious. It was weird but it always felt like people were throwing it in my face that they still had their person, and I didn't. Why couldn't Booby still be here? Why did other people get to have their best friend and I couldn't have mine?

Life After Death

The Rebirth

It took such a long time to start feeling like myself again. Honestly, I still don't feel 100% like the old me. But I vividly remember the day that I decided to start living again.

It was a random day probably four months after booby's death and I was sitting in my room contemplating suicide. I thought to myself: "if I take these pills everything will be over." No more pain. No more misery. I'll be set free. Suddenly, I heard a small voice say, you may be free from your pain if you take these pills. But then what? You'll only end up making things worse. What about your family? Your siblings would lose another big sister. Your mother would have to bury another child. Killing yourself is not the answer. Do you think Shamara would want that?

It wasn't what I wanted to hear. And I repeatedly battled with the thought of taking my life. Things just weren't getting better for me. Even though I hated to admit it, that inner voice was right. Suicide would have caused more harm than good. Destroying myself was not going to bring Shamara back. I was lost in this world. My life had become chaotic, and I got tired of feeling sorry for myself. I thought about my sister, and what she would say if she saw the person that I had become: drinking my days away and contemplating suicide. I knew that she wouldn't want me to give up on life. I wanted to make a change not only for myself but for Shamara.

I couldn't control the fact that she was gone. I lost my best friend and then I lost myself. It didn't feel like I had anything under control anymore. And then it clicked. There was one thing that I still had control over. And that was how I chose to live my life. I could either let life pass me by. Or I could regain my power and make the best of things. I chose to make the best of life. This was the start of me being intentional. The start of me changing my perspective.

One day I was in the basement looking through old books. One of my co-workers bought me a book about grief and I wanted to read it. I thought: hey why not? I have to start my healing process somewhere. As I was looking for the book, I came across a turquoise binder that read "She Rose mentoring program." It was the binder that I created earlier that year for the mentoring program with Sherelle. I had completely forgot about it. The binder consisted of weekly personal and spiritual goals, as well as my daily prayer journals. It had been five months since the program. I decided to look through it. Reading my old journals was interesting. It was so refreshing reading about how content I used to be. I had such strong faith. My days were so peaceful. I possessed the type of confidence that only comes from Christ. I realized that I hadn't talked to God in months. I missed him. I missed the sense of peace that he brought into my life.

Journal Entry

October 2019

Dear Lord, I miss you so much. How are you? I miss our talks. I miss our quality time. I miss how you used to help me believe in myself. I am tired and I'm frustrated. But instead of trying to do things in my own strength I am coming straight to you. I need your help, Father. Today I want to make a change. A change for myself. It's time I get back on track with my prayer life, discipline, and my obedience.

I know that I can do this God but not without your help. I love you. And I pray for your guidance and your strength. Help me to fall in love with you again. Help me to be interested in your word again. You love me and you want what is best for me. But I realize that I have to want what is best for myself as well.

I know that you won't force anything between us. I must be willing to do my part. I miss you so much Father. I want to change, trust me; I do. Please be patient with me and never leave my side.

I was embarrassed to return to God after being away for so long. It reminds me of the story of the prodigal son. Ha! God never wanted me to leave his sight. I knew that my return was anticipated. I was honest with God and I asked for forgiveness. God is so polite and patient. He won't force you to come to him, but he'll always be there waiting for you whenever you are ready. He embraced me like I had never left his side. I began to slowly pray and study the word again. I was intentional about getting in his presence. I was reminded through scripture that I was never alone in my storm. Even though I walk through the darkest valley, I will fear no evil, for you are with me, your rod and your staff they comfort me. Psalms 23.

Even though I felt like I could not go on with life, God's word reminded me that through Christ, I have the power to do anything. Philippians 4:13 says, I can do all things through Christ who strengthens me. The reestablishment of my relationship with God shifted my mindset. Our relationship was built on a solid foundation, so it wasn't difficult finding my way back to him. Even though I physically removed myself from his presence, the love and deep reverence that I felt for the Lord, never left my heart. My relationship with Christ is just like my relationship with my earthly parents. For instance, I'm sure your mom or dad has upset you before. Probably to the point that you wanted to stop talking to them, or you did. Nevertheless, the circumstance didn't stop you from loving them. Although I was angry with God, I never stopped loving him.

I was still heartbroken by Shamara's death, being back in relationship with God didn't cause me to dismiss my feelings. But as my mentor (in my head) Tatum Temia would say, "Acknowledge how you feel and stand on what you know." I acknowledged the fact that I was still mourning. I told God that I was hurt. I felt broken. I didn't understand why this had to happen to my family. But I also had to stand on what I know. The word of God. James 1:2-4 says, Consider it pure joy my brothers and sisters, whenever you face trials of many kinds, because you know that the testing of your faith produces perseverance. Let perseverance finish its work so that you may be mature and complete, not lacking anything. I acknowledged the fact that my sister was gone and that I was fearful of the unknown.

But I stood on Isaiah 41:10 NIV which says: So do not fear for I am with you; do not be dismayed, for I am your God. I will strengthen you and help you. I will uphold you with my righteous right hand. I created a habit of acknowledging my feelings and standing on God's word, this taught me to walk in my authority. Which means knowing the power that I hold through Christ. Regardless of my circumstances God's word always reassured me of my protection.

Creating new habits became second nature to me. If I was going to gain control over my life, I had to be willing to create new habits not only in my relationship with God, but in all areas of my life. I decided to take better care of myself mentally as well as physically. I started by drinking more water. Ha! You probably weren't expecting that to be the first change. For me to operate at my maximum potential, I needed to work on my body from the inside out. That meant changing my lifestyle. I got myself a gym membership, and I dedicated two days a week to a full body workout. Working out wasn't just helpful physically - it was therapeutic. The gym was an outlet for me. Instead of focusing my attention on grief and other life issues; it was a chance for me to relax and clear my mind. Next, I created a morning and nighttime routine. My nightly routine focused solely on getting myself to bed at a decent hour. That meant no activities or events during the week. My motto was Don't ask cuz I ain't going. Catch me on the weekend. I would get home after the gym, take my shower, and turn my phone on do not disturb. I was in bed no later than nine pm. I was adamant about changing the way that I approached each day. From there I began to speak life into myself. Even when I woke up in an unpleasant mood, I would tell myself, "Today will be a good day." Proverbs 18:21 says, the tongue has the power of life and death, and those who love it will eat its fruit. I deliberately spoke against any negative thoughts that came my way. I was not giving life, or anybody in it the opportunity to determine what type of day I would have. I was intentional about creating the type of day that I wanted to have.

I was mindful of the things that I fed my spirit.Especially first thing in the morning and before I went to bed at night. I remember at one point I would wake up, roll over and instantly get on social media. Don't get me wrong, I enjoyed social media but that shouldn't be on anybody's mind first thing in the morning. Social media wasn't feeding my mind anything positive. So, I took another route. I chose to wake up each morning and spend the first few hours with God. My routine wasn't much different from the one in my pruning season. Which consisted of prayer, journaling and reading God's word. Sometimes I incorporated a little worship music.

Journaling was my favorite because it gave me a chance to be still. It gave me a chance to start my day in a positive way by expressing my gratitude. Taking care of my well-being (working out, resting, and creating daily routines) gave me structure. I started to feel much better. Grieving was still a challenge, of course. But for the first time in months, I no longer felt like my life was spiraling out of control. Even though I felt better, I had moments when I wanted to revert to my old habits. I missed sitting on the couch drinking and feeling sorry for myself because it was easy, and it didn't require effort. I had to remember that I wasn't that person anymore. We have to understand that when God transitions us into a new season of life, we cannot shrink into the old versions of ourselves.A new season required me to operate at a different level. I couldn't carry that same negative mindset into the next season of my life. Although I was uncomfortable, I had to embrace the woman that I had become. Redefining who I was in a season where I didn't recognize myself; required effort.

As I was writing the "Losing myself" chapter, I was certain that it was the most difficult season for me. But honestly it wasn't. Nothing is challenging about giving up. It requires minimal effort. The rebirth was the most challenging for me. Learning how to live again after experiencing the most traumatic season of my life; required effort.

When it appears I had nothing to live for; changing my perspective took effort. Seeking God when I no longer wanted to believe; took effort. It took the kind of faith that I only saw in my great grandparents. The kind of strength that I only see in women twice my age. When most people would have quit, due to life's unforeseen circumstances, I kept fighting. How was I able to overcome my adversity? How was I able to take everything that life threw my way, and keep my sanity? God. That's all. That's it. There is no secret code or formula. I like to think that my conviction, and the relationship that I build with God was my preparation. It was preparation for the life changing season that I was getting ready to enter. The storm wasn't meant to break me, it was sent to rebuild me. I had no idea what I was getting ready to experience but God did. If God wouldn't have come into my life in January of 2019, I may not have survived losing my sister. Because I was a different person then. With a different perspective. Mentally I wasn't strong enough. God coming into my life and changing who I thought I was, is the reason I am still here today.

I see a lot of people on social media making jokes about how they don't believe in God. And to each his own. I'm not here to judge. But what's the harm in believing in God? I could understand if God were telling us to live by a harmful set of rules. But the bible is literally a book of principles that help you gain value and structure. In my opinion, living by these rules help us, more than they harm us. Think about it, life is difficult. Problems will always arise. We can't just be out here winging it. Thinking that we can do everything in our own strength. No matter who you are there will come a time in your life when a problem is too much for you to handle on your own. Who do you turn to? What keeps you focus? What keeps you sane? When an issue becomes overwhelming. And your momma can't fix it. Your girl/man can't fix it. Your friends can't fix it. Who do you turn to? I'm not saying that everybody needs to believe in God. I'm saying if you don't believe in God, you definitely need to believe in some form of higher power.

I had a few different plans for my life. Plan B if my plan A didn't work out. And a plan C, just in case my plan B. fell through. But never did I think that God would intervene. I never thought that God could use me. It is by the grace of God that I am still here. I was gracefully broken not for my sake. But so that God can get the glory. I was gracefully broken so that when people read my story and see that I made it out; they find strength in knowing that they can too.

Grief, Now

Living in a world without Shamara is difficult. Like a baby learning to take their first steps, or a teenager learning to drive for the first time. I am uncomfortable. I sometimes wish that grief came with a manual. Because it's so overwhelming trying to navigate life once you've experienced grieving.

When I hear the statement, "Time heals all wounds" I cringe. That doesn't apply to my grief. No amount of time will ever heal my broken heart. It's been two years since Shamara passed away. Although my grieving process looks a lot different, I am still hurting. Grieving for me is taking life one day at a time. It's me being patient with myself. Grieving is me embracing the fact that my emotions are unpredictable. I could go a full week without crying, without being angry and without questioning my sisters' death. And the following week may be the complete opposite. My soul is still in agony, but I have decided not to run from my pain. I had to wake up one day and choose to be intentional. I remember thinking, she was too young to die. She was only twenty-seven years old. Why her? The question still lingers in my head. But I've accepted the fact that these are questions that I'll never have the answers to. I'm not always successful, but I try to stay out of my head because it leads to overthinking. I realize that if I stay in my thoughts, I may drive myself crazy. Or worse, I could possibly send myself into a depressive state. I don't like to think that everything happens for a reason. I find comfort in reassuring myself that in life things happen, and unfortunately, there won't always be an explanation as to why. It may sound crazy but it's better than overthinking something that I have no control over.

Beforehand, I was fearful of the unknown. But now I truly believe that I am okay to go on with life. Now, when I see other people out with their sisters or best friends, I'm slow to become angry. Instead, I think of how blessed they are. I wonder if they cherish the bond that they've created. I wonder if they realize how special life's moments are. These days, when my strength is complimented, I smile and nod. No longer do I allow myself to get upset. Instead, I say thank you and I thank God that I don't look like what I've been through.

Life is still a challenge for me but, again, I am patient with myself. I recently found a therapist to help me work through my trauma. Talking about what I've been through has helped me evolve. I had a difficult time embracing my emotions, but therapy has challenged me to work through them. I find it soothing to cry whenever I need to. I'll even play music that reminds me of Shamara, just so I can cry. Whenever she crosses my mind, I embrace those thoughts. I laugh out loud at old jokes. I reminisce on conversations that we had, and I smile to myself. Grieving is a process but being intentional about working through your grief is another process within itself. It's painful but it's possible. To anybody going through the grieving process, hold on to your memories and keep fighting! Every day that you are alive is worth living.

Final Thoughts

Everything in life has a process. But society likes to make people think that "A Process" doesn't exist. People only give you bits and pieces of their story. They show you who they used to be and who they are today, without showing you the hard work and sacrifice. And that's because the process ain't pretty. It's usually not fun or full of glitz and glamour. As you can see my process wasn't pretty, but what I love most about it is that it manifested a different version of me. A version of myself that I had no idea I could be. I didn't think that I was capable of handling the pressure that life put on me. But I handled it with grace. Everything that I have gone through is still an ongoing process. Grief, my relationship with God, and my mental health. One of the key aspects of my ongoing process is not putting more on myself than I can handle. It's also the key to my perseverance. I've grown so much over the past two years, and it frustrates me to think that my growth was dependent on my sister's death. It may seem strange but it's hard for me not to look at it that way.

Ironically, sometimes the things that we go through in life are not about us. I may have overcome this situation to save someone else's life. I may have been fighting for my life so that someone else doesn't have to fight for theirs. When I look at my circumstance from this perspective it gives me hope. It gives me hope to know that my story may be attached to someone else's survival.

ACKNOWLEDGMENTS

I want to start by giving honor to God. I thank you for never leaving my side, for showing up during the storm and for restoring my faith. Thank you for our talks and your guidance. I thank you for giving me this vision for my book. You helped me find purpose in my pain. I am forever grateful. I love you.

To my mommy: you are my heart, I thank you for never giving up on me. You helped me grow by allowing me to make my own mistakes. But no matter what, you have always been supportive. I thank you for your transparency and your wisdom. You have taught me to be true to who I am. The respect that I have for you is immense. You are the light of my life, my protection and best friend. I am so thankful that over the years I not only got to experience you as my mom, but as a friend and mentor. I love you forever.

To LaKyra, my baby sister, thank you for being such a sweet and beautiful person from the inside out. You are one of my best friends. Your love is genuine and pure, and I couldn't have asked God for a better little sister. Thank you for understanding and accepting me. Thank you for your strength and allowing me to be vulnerable in your presence. Continue to let your light shine. Embrace the young woman that you have become. Big sis will always be here to make you laugh, give you advice, and get on your nerves. I cherish our bond. You mean the world to me. I love you.

Davon, my favorite brother, thank you for being a true friend. I appreciate every moment that you listen to me vent, every time that you read over a piece of my manuscript and give your advice. You are truly wise beyond your years and that's one of the things that I love most about you. Continue to defeat the odds and thrive. I am proud of you. I'll always be here to pour into you and lift your spirits. Remember to create your own path and dominate. I love you.

ACKNOWLEDGMENTS

To my great-grandparents, thank you Mr. & Mrs. Jones for all that you have instilled in me. Thank you for introducing me to God's love and his word at such an early age. You set the foundation for my faith. I miss you both dearly. I hope that I am making you proud.

To my sisters, Ashley (Ash bash), Desire (Rae), Desiree, (Ree), Jasmine (Mook) and Kaitlyn (Kattie). Thank you for your support, your loyalty, and respect. I love you all from the bottom of my heart. At my darkest hour, you were there to comfort and encourage me. You were there for me when I was too broken to be there for myself. I appreciate the visits, the phone calls, and the text messages. Because of you I was able to make it through the most traumatic season of my life. Your selflessness, your love, and your huge hearts are greatly appreciated. Thank you all for showing me what friendship looks like. I try my best every day to be as good of a friend to all as you have been to me. I will always be here for you.

Thank you, Marlena, for being my accountability partner. Thank you for your encouraging words & for being here to listen whenever I need you. We've grown so much together. I thank God for our relationship. I want you to know that you are exactly where God wants you to be. Embrace your process. I love you. And I appreciate you more than you will ever know.

To My Meyers Lab family

Especially Erin, Latrice, Shelly, LaKeisha and Tameka. I thank you all for the advice, encouraging words and resources. On the days when I had to face the world, regardless of what I was going through, I could always count on you all to help me get through. I love and appreciate you so much. I am so glad that God brought each of you into my life. There is no way I would have been able to make it through some of those tough days without you all. Thank you from the bottom of my heart for the tremendous amount of support. My girls for life.

Dealing with Grief: 7 ways to cope

Now I know you're probably thinking "sis, it's nothing you can tell me that will take away this pain that I'm feeling." And you're right. Dealing with death is hard. It may even seem impossible. Nothing I say can justify the pain that you may be feeling. I know because I've been there. There were no words that could have been said. No book that I could have read. Not even a therapist that I could have talked to that would have made my pain go away. Believe me, I tried. During my grieving process, I didn't care to hear any of that stuff. I'm aware that I can't get rid of your pain. So, I won't try. I will, however, give you advice on how to deal with what you are feeling. I want to share with you a few things that would have been helpful for me to know during my grieving process. Disclaimer: You must be willing to do the work that is required in order for the process to be effective.

1. DO NOT rush the process.

You cannot rush the grieving process. Don't expect to get over your grief overnight. You won't always be in the state that you were in when the loss first happened. But you will more than likely always grieve the loss of that person. There should be no pressure for you to rush through what you are dealing with. Take your time because grief can be a lifelong process. You cannot fast forward your emotions. You must be willing to take life one day at a time.

2. Release your emotions.

Grief causes an overflow of emotions Fear, sadness, anger - just to name a few. It's unhealthy to suppress these emotions. Instead release them.

Cry whenever you feel the need to. Be angry because you have every right to be. Yell and scream if you need to. Sometimes communicating your emotions could help you release them. Find a safe and healthy way to rid yourself of all the emotions that you may be feeling.

3. Seek help/support.

Everybody needs somebody. Especially while grieving. Grief is a heavy burden to deal with. It's necessary to have someone supporting you in your time of need. This could be family, friends or even a therapist. Now I know I stated earlier that a therapist could not make my pain go away. Which was true. But I was seeking therapy with the wrong intentions. Therapy was never meant to make our pain, suffering and/or trauma disappear. Therapy is used to treat, relieve, and or heal. I encourage therapy. A listening ear makes a difference. You may not even want to talk. You may just want to sit in silence and enjoy someone's company. Either way you should not try to get through the grieving process alone.

4. Take care of yourself.

This can be challenging especially when you are in the midst of your grief. You neglect a lot of things unconsciously during the grieving process. As a result, your physical and mental health may suffer. You may even get to a point where you can't sleep, you have no desire to eat, shower or do anything for that matter. Take a walk to get fresh air and clear your head. Journal your thoughts. Stay hydrated and eat properly. Take your friends up on that offer to get out of the house. Sometimes activities and hobbies can help you take your mind off the pain that grief causes.

5. There is no right or wrong way to grieve.

Grief is unique. Your grieving process may be different from someone else's. You may spend your days sad, frustrated, and isolated. While someone else may be crying one day and the next day they are laughing and enjoying life. Grief is unpredictable. And that's okay. How grief shows up depends on you as a person and how you may or may not be feeling in that moment. It is important that we recognize and respect the fact that everybody has their own way of grieving.

6. DO NOT let grief win.

It is necessary that you take all the time that you need to grieve. I told you before to cry, be angry and frustrated when you need to be. But what I need you to know is that you CAN NOT stay there. Staying in a state of anger, frustration and sadness may lead to self - destruction. This next piece of advice will require you to be intentional. After you've taken the time that you need to get through the grieving stages you have to choose life. You must choose to get up every day and keep fighting. You can't let the fact that you are grieving take over your life. You can't let grief win.

7. Be patient with yourself.

We live in a society that thrives off instant gratification. We expect everything to happen quick, fast, and in a hurry. Real life issues don't go away as quickly as they come. Be patient with yourself. Remember that you shared a relationship with the person that you've lost. This person meant something to you. Therefore, it will take time for you to accept the fact that they are no longer with us. Be patient with yourself because you've never met this version of you before.

www.ingramcontent.com/pod-product-compliance
Lightning Source LLC
Chambersburg PA
CBHW032133090426
42743CB00007B/582